Finding Brand

The Brand Book Tutorial

Finding Brand

The Brand Book Tutorial

Tisha R. Oehmen

A Paradux Media Group Book

Finding Brand: The Brand Book Tutorial

Published by Paradux Media Group
© Copyright 2013 by Tisha R. Oehmen
Editing by Brian Boone
Graphic Design by Kelly Congleton and Tara Sloan

First Printing 2013

ISBN-10: 0615876021
ISBN-13: 978-0615876023

- Finding Brand website: FindingBrand.com
- Paradux Media Group website: ParaduxMedia.com
- Tisha Oehmen's website: TishaOehmen.com

DEDICATION

For Michael, who always believed this was possible and without whom this never would have been written. I wouldn't change a thing.

For Chloe, Ezra, and Jackson, faithful companions, writing buddies, comic relief, and enforced writing breaks. Thank you for your unconditional love and companionship, and most of all, for keeping it all in perspective.

ACKNOWLEDGMENTS

This book would not have been possible without the love, help, and support of my partner, Michael Frey. It also would not have been possible without the team members at Paradux Media Group: Mike Frey, Kelly Congleton, and Dixie Nuñez, and our many co-workers.

This book would never have been written without the support and encouragement of my good friends, Carmen Voillequé, Cynthia Couch, Angela Peacor, Kellie Hill, and Loren Fogelman.

Thank you all for your endless encouragement, patience, and nudging. This book would not exist without you.

"It's the not-yet in the now,
the taste of fruit that does not-yet exist
hanging the blossom on the bough."

~Laurens Van der Post

TABLE OF CONTENTS

LIST OF FIGURES

INTRODUCTION

Certain brands become synonymous with their products—"Kleenex" means the same thing as "tissue," and "Xerox" the same as "photocopy," for example. Ever wonder how some brands are able to achieve that? Or how others simply do not? Or how one business can be on the tip of everyone's tongues, while another fades quietly into obscurity?

The secret is branding. If you took two businesses with the same business model, pricing, and location, and one pursued a tight branding strategy, while the other did whatever felt right, nine times out of 10 you would see the business that practiced good branding is the one that would succeed.

Businesses that pay attention to their branding understand what is being offered to its customers. Those businesses are dogged in their determination to provide it, and they make decisions in accordance with bringing the business ever closer to the goal. Everything they do, internally and externally, is in pursuit of their brand. In other words, the brand becomes genetically encoded upon the business. The business had no alternative but to become successful; for smart businesses that want to succeed, it's about Finding Brand.

Finding Brand

The Brand Book Tutorial

THE STRATEGY OF BRANDING

WHAT IS A BRAND?

What is a Brand? is a question that isn't often asked aloud, but one that I suspect is often on people's minds. They're just too embarrassed to ask.

There are lots of answers to this question, Marketing Accountability Standards Board (American Marketing Association) endorses the following definition as part of its ongoing "Common Language: Marketing Activities and Metrics" project.

> A brand is a "name, term, design, symbol, or any other feature that identifies one seller's good or service as distinct from those of other sellers."

Branding is about creating instant recognition in the consumer's mind. It can be something as simple as a voice, a graphic, or a phrase. While these definitions are partially accurate, they fail to fully communicate the answer to the question, **What is a Brand?** Branding is more than just a name, term, design, or symbol; there is something more — an innate emotional component. Consultant Daryl Travis, author of *Emotional Branding*, gets us a little closer to the answer: "A brand isn't a brand to you until it develops an emotional connection with you." (Travis 2000)

Travis is right. At its heart, branding is about creating an emotional resonance with a brand — ideally a positive emotional resonance. A strong brand should invoke instant, favorable, emotion. Marty Neumeier, the author of The Brand Gap, goes on to explain, "a brand is a person's gut feeling about a product, service, or company." (Neumeier 2005)

We're getting closer to the real answer, but there is still something more to a brand. Perhaps my favorite answer comes from Fred Burt of Siegel+Gale: **"A brand is a reason to choose."** (Slattery 2010)

That's it. It's so simple, yet so complex. What is a Brand? "A brand is a reason to choose. "

That's why branding is so important in marketing. Branding gives people a reason to choose:

- your product over your competitor's
- your business over the business down the street
- to invest themselves in your success.

Your brand has the capacity to ensure your company's success or lack thereof. So pay attention to it. Build it. And most of all, share the story every chance you get.

WHY BRAND?

Branding is a long process. It's not easy, it costs money, and it doesn't create immediate traffic. Many times along this journey to a great brand, you will have to remind yourself why you are embarking on this endeavor at all. When those moments hit, just remember that a great brand is critical to your success.

When it comes to making a choice to try a business, a consumer naturally run through a "consideration set" from which they choose. Try this: Off the top of your head, list three dinner spots. Got them? Good. Those three spots you just listed are your consideration set.

It's important for a business to land in its target audience's consideration set because they are most likely to choose from one of the first three places they think of. To continue the example from above, if the restaurant wasn't in your top three, then they're not getting your dinner business tonight.

The purpose and goal of branding is to get your business into the "top three." You want your business to be on someone's consideration set when they're ready to go out for dinner, buy a new car, or find a new insurance agent; you want your business to be thought about. There are no two ways about it — it's a long-term investment. The good news is that if you're doing the work, creating a compelling position, and creating alignment with the brand for your business, it will all pay off in the long run. In fact, a study by Booz Allen Hamilton/Wolff Olins determined that "Brand-guided companies significantly outperform their rivals." (Harter, et al. 2005) Now that's powerful!

Back when I was doing marketing in the world of finance, and young in my marketing career, I had the privilege of working with a brilliant marketing firm. The principal there assured me that by the end of the year (it was January), everyone in the city would be able to name my financial institution in a list of three. We spent a lot of money on branding, particularly in fostering a great deal of what he called "likeability," and at the end of the year, he was right — people did indeed list us in their consideration set. To be fair, we were not an unknown entity in January, we were an established brand, nor did we have people knocking down our doors in December to open a checking account. But our business steadily increased, and the top-of-mind awareness we bought with our brand recognition was critical to our ongoing growth and success.

Finance is a lot like other service-based businesses. It takes a lot to get someone to switch to another provider. It's a hassle, it's a pain, and for the end consumer, the benefits are often not dramatic. So the key for a service-based business is, at the very least, to be on the consideration set. That way, when the consumer is ready to make a change, they're ready to make a change to you.

That's why you're spending all this time, energy, and money on creating a great brand: so that you can reap the benefits the next time someone gets fed up with who they are doing business with and is ready to try someone new.

THE POWER OF BRAND

Marketing and advertising experts tell us that we are supposed to "brand," and as marketers, we even feel the rightness of branding in our bones. After all, who wouldn't want a name like Nike, Kleenex, or Starbucks to call their own? But folks in business often find that branding is expensive and know that it won't always produce the immediate results that a "low, low price sale" will.

Yet that is the exact moment when spending money and energy building a brand will allow your company to leap over the competition. The good news is that you do not have to take the traditional approach of spending lots of money in order to identify and build your brand. You have all the tools you need available to you already, and at little or no cost.

First, do not be fooled that you need some high priced focus group and long-term study, before you can begin to brand yourself. Let's face it — *you* know what your company is about. *You* know what it stands for. *You* know what values you held when you created it. *You* know why you believed the business would be successful. No one knows it better than *you*!

A good brand can help catapult a business to success. But a great brand, well executed, is more than just marketing. A great brand will incorporate every element of a company's belief system into a tangible concept. Your brand should start with your company's mission and vision, be rooted in your company's values, be steeped in your company's culture, and finally be evident in all internal and external language and visual elements. At the end of the day, "Effective corporate branding will come with dedication to honest self-assessment, responsive attitudes toward stakeholders, and respect for the values that attract all parties to the corporation." (Hatch and Schultz 2003)

Putting in the time, energy, and effort to genetically encode a brand in a business is considerable — it's not easy, and it's not for the faint of heart. But just as genetic encoding can deliver a migrating bird to the same pond year after year after traveling hundreds of miles, so too can consistent positioning deliver customers day after day, month after month, and year after year. That's the power of an effective brand.

Developing the brand is hard work to be sure. But it's not impossible, and it's not only for those with massive budgets and or a huge staff. All businesses are improved by having a brand. And with a little time and effort, anyone can create an amazing brand.

That is what we're going to do in this book. Chapter by chapter, step by step, exercise by exercise, we're going to create a world-class brand for your company, or even just for you. No one's pretending that genetically encoding your brand on your business is going to be easy, but the results are more than worth the effort. This book can help!

THE SECRET TO A GREAT BRAND

A highlight of the 1991 movie *City Slickers* was the enigmatic and wise cowboy, Curly. Over the course of the movie, Curly revealed that the secret to life is just one thing; the "trick" was figuring out what that "one thing" was.

Curly's wisdom applies not just to life, but also to business and marketing. When a company chooses to focus its time and energy on just one thing, what can be accomplished is magnified and enhanced. The results become exponentially greater because of the focus and single-mindedness.

The secret to a great brand is *One Thing — just One Thing.*

No question; it will take discipline and fortitude to choose the "one thing" your brand stands for. Allowing your brand to be distracted, taken off course, and generally waylaid is far, far easier than maintaining your allegiance to just that One Thing.

I met recently with a local chapter of a national non-profit organization. As is true for most non-profits with national affiliations, this organization raised money for its national charitable fund, as well as its local charitable fund. (If you are keeping count that is two things). The local organization also wanted to demonstrate its commitment to the local community and give away money to other non-profits in the region. (That's three things). Now, in good economic times when the non-profit is riding a popularity high, with lots of money coming in, there's enough money to go around and support all three of its goals. But when times are a little tougher, three things is two too many things to focus on. There isn't enough money to go around, and unless this organization makes some difficult decisions about what the brand stands for, they will be unable to support all three charitable goals.

The bigger problem, however, is that the local chapter's membership and potential membership doesn't have a clear understanding of the chapter's reason for being—its brand. The chapter struggles with its identity and providing potential donors a reason to join this chapter over others. In failing to stand for something, their brand has utterly failed to stand for anything. The root of the problem is simple to explain, but almost impossible to change.

The inability to focus doesn't just happen to non-profits—it happens to every brand that loses focus of its "One Thing." Normal elements of business, such as changes in staffing, pursuing business expansion opportunities, and meeting community needs can all have the potential to throw a business off its One Thing.

When that happens, unless the organization has the fortitude to check itself and return to its one thing—or have the guts to step away from its old One Thing and create a new One Thing—then the organization will slowly slip away from its customers' minds and their buying patterns. One thing — and sticking to it — that's the secret to a great brand.

Strategy and Branding

In business, we call the single-minded focus on just One Thing, "Strategy." When you are operating the business and the marketing department from a place of focused strategy, the results become exponentially greater.

The path to well executed strategy involves every aspect of the business, and it occurs at every level of the organization. Many books, articles, and blog posts have been written about how to permeate strategy throughout a business, but one of the most concise comes from Kaplan and Norton in their book, *The Strategy-Focused Organization*. They suggest the following five steps:

1. Translate the strategy into operational terms.

2. Align the organization to the strategy.

3. Make strategy everyone's everyday job.

4. Make strategy a continual process.

5. Mobilize change through executive leadership. (Kaplan and Norton 2000)

While these steps are appropriate for permeating strategy throughout an organization, they're also the steps that are necessary for infusing a brand throughout the same organization. There is considerable power to be found in synchronizing all the outbound messages together into one cogent, synthesized idea.

Imagine the unity of message that could occur if your salespeople were selling the same thing your print advertising was selling. And if your print advertisement looked like your website, which looked like your social media profiles and direct mail and email messages. Then imagine that the radio spot sounded like the TV spot, which all looked similar to the print advertising and website.

Sounds intuitive, right? Unfortunately, that level of message synchronizing rarely occurs for even the largest, most sophisticated brands. But it's something that is worth paying attention to and striving toward. And the good news is that it's something that can be more easily accomplished for small and mid-sized businesses than it is for those very large, very sophisticated brands.

How do you get a synchronized outward facing message to help your customers to focus on what you want them to focus on? It often starts by truly understanding your brand position and how your brand position is influenced by (and influencing) your business strategy.

One exceptional way to become intimately acquainted with your brand is to create a "brand book." The process of creating one, as well as the end product of a document to reference, will help to create single-minded focus on your brand and strategy that will result in enhanced sales and increased profitability for your company.

BRANDING VIA A BRAND BOOK

The brand book is the quintessential guidebook that will help a business to align its internal and external practices to help it to reach its goals. A brand book is more than just a marketing department tool. It should be *the* guiding internal document that guides employees and stakeholders in every action. It should be the culmination of all internal and external thinking; it should be a business's DNA map, the tangible representation of all the genetic encoding that makes your business unique and special.

Creating a brand book is one way to really work through each and every aspect of the creation of your new brand position and to ensure that your entire team gets on board with the brand position. Whether you create it yourself, or whether you hire someone to do it, putting in the time and energy to create your own brand book will help to solidify what your brand stands for.

Creating a brand book isn't easy work. It's often tedious to put together, usually represents significant internal negotiation, and most of all, it embodies a willingness to dedicate the company, stakeholders, customers, and vendors to properly "following the rules" about the brand.

WHAT MAKES A SUCCESSFUL BRAND BOOK?

The whole purpose behind a brand book is to help keep the business goals and brand consistent as it is used by an ever-increasing number of people. As such, brand books try to define and quantify the brand in ways that would help both those unfamiliar and familiar with the brand to understand it, use it properly, and maintain "the integrity of the brand." The act of creating a brand book will do two very important things for your business and brand identity:

1. **A brand book helps to create a brand.** A brand book will help you to flesh out what your brand identity stands for in a meaningful way. The very act of completing the exercises necessary to create the brand book will help you, and your business, learn something important about your core values, belief structure, and what is and is not acceptable within the company culture. With every new page of the brand book you create, you will learn something new about your brand identity that you never considered.

2. **A brand book helps others understand your brand.** The brand book will articulate, in easy to digest ways, exactly what your company stands for. It will distill the past and the future, blending company history, strategy, with the way the you intend to get there. The brand book is quite literally your roadmap for future decisions, large and small and the basis for every decision that your business makes going forward.

THE BRAND BOOK IS MORE THAN JUST A MARKETING TOOL

The brand book should be *the* reference document for your organization. It should be the one…

- that people carry around
- that decision-makers consult before making a decision
- that informs employee disciplinary decisions
- that dictates (and demonstrates how) customers should be treated
- that sets the tone for how your organization functions

I know, that sounds like the Strategic Plan. While it's true that elements of both should be identical, the brand book should be written in such a way that corporate secrets are not disclosed, five- and 10-year goals not articulated, and key metrics not covered. In short, the brand book is the map and compass that help you get where you are going, but it's not turn-by-turn instructions on how to get there.

All that being said, however, a brand book can help the marketing department become more efficient with both time and money. It can help the training department to be "on message" with regard to how customers are to be treated. It can help management make decisions in accordance with their stated goals. And, perhaps most importantly, it helps every employee to understand what the business is trying to accomplish, as well as their role in it.

When everyone is using the brand in the same way, the brand grows bigger and faster with less effort than could be imagined. A brand book, when it is well executed, does provide a tremendous amount of insight in the brand.

- It should be accessible and understandable for every employee in the business.
- It should be a reference guide for business partners, ad agencies, website designers, employees, executives, and volunteers.
- It should be the business's creation, essence, and brand distilled down so that the complete story and all the relevant parts are included in one place.
- It should be more than just something you share with marketing partners. A brand book should make the ideal gift for a new employee joining the business, to truly understand the brand position and values of the business.

Creating a brand book is a tangible declaration that your business takes itself seriously and intends to become successful. The brand book will become the codification of your brand, the visual, verbal, and behavioral expressions of your business model (Knox and Bickerton 2003). It will help internal staff alignment as well as external customer understanding. Most of all, it will provide a solid foundation upon which to build the business.

Your brand book will not ensure your company's longevity, but it will certainly help. The clearer you are about your business, what it stands for, and how it should be represented in your community, the more likely it is that you will be able to make smart business decisions that build on each other and create synergy, which leads to better results.

BRAND BOOK TUTORIAL

THE HEAVENS PARTED

When I was just starting out in marketing at the financial institution, my boss asked me to work with our Marketing Agency to create a brand book, and I still remember – to this day – the awe and sparkle that accompanied the words "brand book" when he gave me my new goal. It was as if there was something semi-holy about it. Certainly, it wasn't something that any ordinary marketing person could create. No, it had to be created by "the Marketing Agency." And getting the brand book written was expensive, extensive, and exhausting. With more than a year's lead-time, we almost did not get it written by the deadline.

The day it finally arrived, the proverbial heavens parted, a beam of light shown down from the sky, and "The Brand Book" was delivered.

This brand book was thick. It was easily 100 pages, and technical, esoteric, academic, and pretentious—how could it not be?— and it was … BORING! Seriously, to read that version of the brand book cover-to-cover would make even a marketing addict's eyes glaze over and cure the most significant case of insomnia. What's worse? Let's face it—the only person at that business (or any other) that would ever bother to read (and struggle through) the brand book cover to cover was me, the person whose job it was to have it written.

Since we know that there is a higher purpose for a brand book, the question becomes, "How do you write a useful brand book, and not spend all your time creating a doorstop that never gets opened read or used?"

The answer is that you can't fully outsource this very intimate expression of your business. You have to be *involved.* You have to be *accountable.* Most of all, you are going to have to engage others throughout the organization in this process. This is a document born of the marketing department, but without the full backing of the entire management and stakeholder structure, it will not be nearly as successful as it might otherwise have been.

So how do you go about actually writing a brand book? Well, that's one of the things we'll be covering. We're going to progress through creating a brand and the writing of a brand book, step-by-step. Best used, this book should be a companion piece as you write your very own brand book.

Take your time, really work the exercises. Be sure to share the results of each exercise with your boss, management team, and other key stakeholders as you go. Writing a brand book in a vacuum will only ensure that one of two things will happen: 1) You'll end up re-writing the brand book with input from those individuals after that fact, or 2) The brand book will become just another book that sits on a shelf – unused and unreferenced in your office. So share it *in progress,* and adjust and incorporate the ideas your stakeholders share with you. It needs to be a document representing the businesses—not just your ideology.

Pick your pace, and stick to it. The reason most brand books never are completed is that they do require a lot of work. They ask a lot of the authors. And let's face it; some of the exercises are *hard.* So right now, pick your pace and commit to it. Are you going to do one chapter a week? Every other day? Once a month? It doesn't matter. As long as you are making forward progress and can mark on a calendar when you will have your brand book completed.

Finally, remember that this is *your* brand book. If you don't like one of the representations of the brand laid out in this book, it's okay to skip it. If you've got another important piece to your company that I haven't covered, by all means, include it! There is no such thing as a perfect brand book; there is only *your* brand book.

By the time we're done, you'll have a complete and professional brand book that you can share within your business and with valued partners and stakeholders. Most importantly, it won't be used as a glorified doorstop.

BRAND NARRATIVE

To begin the job of creating a brand book, it's important to note that wherever we start, we're going to inevitably come back around at the end and edit what we started to create one cohesive message. The very act of creating a brand book will inform and enhance the brand. Vicious circle? Definitely! Should that stop you from getting started? Not a chance!

The best place to start is to start with the beginning—literally. One of the first pages of the brand book should be dedicated to the history of the brand. This doesn't need to be an exhaustive history, but rather the highlights that lend context and depth to the brand discussed for the duration of the brand book and to begin to frame a position. As you're writing your history, it's critical to pay attention to constructing the foundations of the brand position. The brand will be more authentic and transparent if it springs from its official history, rather than as a contrived marketing position that an agency has created.

IT STARTS WITH A STORY

For thousands of years, humans have utilized stories to provide context, meaning, and a *raison d'être*. Our world is constructed of personal, community, institutional, and political narratives. Think for a moment about the power narrative has played in your life today. Chances are pretty high that upon arriving at work this morning, you met a colleague and shared with them some small tidbit about your week, evening, or even your morning commute. And in that sharing, you created a narrative and a shared moment, where the listener added to their knowledge about you, and the story itself began to define you, not just for the listener, but also for yourself. It may have been funny, sad, tragic, or mundane, but it was a story nonetheless.

You didn't mean to have that affect talking about the traffic jam this morning? It's okay—it's what humans do. We create narratives, and our lives are a series of narratives. And because narratives hold such power, we cannot afford to overlook them as a method for creating common ground when introducing a new idea, product, project, or leveraging a brand.

THE POWER OF A BRAND NARRATIVE

There is considerable power in a brand narrative as a tool for aligning stakeholders and creating consistent messaging. In my experience, a good brand narrative is the incomparable force multiplier. This is because people naturally want to be part of something bigger, they want to matter, and they want their lives to have meaning. Most of all, they want to become part of a gripping narrative. Allowing stakeholders, employees, and even consumers to become part of that brand narrative is the secret to success.

"Because stories are such potent communication tools, telling the story of the corporate brand can be an important and meaningful way to relate the company to its stakeholders." (Hatch and Schultz 2003). With a consistent and compelling brand narrative, employees become ambassadors for your brand and products, stakeholders promote them, earned media becomes easier to earn and, perhaps most importantly, you can create buzz within the industry and attract target audiences. And it's as easy as telling a story.

The first step to telling your story is to take the time to gather all of your relevant source documents. Go on a scavenger hunt for all informative documents about what your business is about. Check your website, even your employee handbook. At a minimum, these source documents should include:

- Mission
- Vision
- Values
- Behavioral standards
- Driving force
- Strategic plan
- Core competencies
- Strategic goals
- Balanced scorecard
- Previously compiled historical documents
- Logo(s), current and prior
- Tagline(s), current and prior
- Any other marketing materials you can find.

Once you've got all your information compiled, review it, really look deep for the common threads, and the threads that stand out and detract from the overall brand position.

When creating your brand book, focus on what the story of your business is. What is the great journey your business is undertaking? What are the interesting details of the story? Why is the world better because your company came along?

An easy way to think of your brand is to understand that it's the story of your business. It's about the history of your business, it's about you as a protagonist and about the evils you battle in this, and it's about your friends and coworkers. How you tell and retell this story defines your business. We all live our stories—your business is no different.

One way to force yourself to tell a compelling tale is to find a young person, seven or eight years old, and tell them your brand story— complete with voices of the good guys and the bad guys and with the climax of the showdown between good (your company) and evil. If you hold their attention, you have the makings of a great brand story.

EXAMPLES

Below are a few examples of the ways brands have chosen to tell their stories in brand books to spark your imagination.

British Airways created a history for their brand book, sharing their story in an interesting and compelling manner. The goal of this portion of their brand book is not only to educate, but also to pull through their heritage to the present day and to engage current stakeholders in delivering that tradition to their customers on a daily basis.

> Our heritage: There can be few world-class companies that boast the heritage and traditions inherent in the British Airways brand. Indeed, the company that became British Airways operated the world's first commercial airline. From the early days of aviation, through to more recent times, our reputation for professionalism and high standards of quality has been second to none. The British Airways name has remained constant since 1974 and has become a byword for the expression of quality travel in the UK, as well as a respected leader in air travel, worldwide. (British Airways 2007, 8)

The brand book of the American Heart Association/American Stroke Association covers their unique story, their reason for being, and sets up the story of how they improve the lives of those they touch. It sets the tone for the rest of their brand book.

> Countless Americans owe their lives to scientific breakthroughs from American Heart Association-funded research and professional guidelines, training, advocacy and programs. Now they use the AHA/ASA to educate and empower themselves so they can give back, feel good about contributing, and save lives by helping others – and future

generations – live healthier, longer lives. (American Heart Association/ American Stroke Association n.d., 9)

The City of Sydney, Australia, simply told a story and humanized the region. They put it together in context with both the past and the future they're trying to create. And they shared a little bit of their brand personality in the process.

> The Redfern area encompassing Redfern, Waterloo, Darlington and Eveleigh is undergoing significant change. The population has become a diverse community with a wide social mix through a range of housing development and socio-economic factors.
>
> There has been a recent increase in cultural activities, new business development and major refurbishments including National Centre of Indigenous Excellence, Redfern Street, Rabbitohs Football and Leagues Club, Channel 7 and the Redfern Park and Oval. Redfern has the potential to become a thriving inner city destination that embraces its past, present and future.
>
> The Redfern brand aims to promote the Redfern area as a destination that is welcoming and vibrant—both for the local and wider community.
>
> The Redfern brand is an opportunity to unify the precinct and help build a strong community spirit. The objective of the brand is to function as a lens through which every marketing, public relations activity and customer interaction embodies a unified vision of fresh energy, revitalisation, professionalism and character—consistent with the businesses and local residents that live in the precinct. (City of Sydney 2010, 3)

The story of Skype (Skype n.d.) clearly articulates both its history and positions Skype as the protagonist in the story, all while also introducing the reader to its unique brand voice, which is casual, humorous, enlightened, and utterly, completely Skype's own.

> Skype is a piece of software that allows people around the world to talk to each other for free. Sure, we've heard this all before. As a company, we're all used to that notion. But then Mister Wu, Smith and Blanc aren't. They may know nothing about Skype. For all we know, they may think the name is some sort of sexually transmitted disease, pyramid scheme or a car made in deepest, darkest Bohemia.
>
> So once again, Skype is for the people. Skype is everything that a teleco is not: generous, interested and proactive. We allow people to talk each other and the world for free.
>
> That will always be news. (Skype n.d., 12-13)

The Kellogg School of Management creates a compelling story in its brand book that invites the reader to join them on its quest. It lays out what students, faculty, and staff will find different about their school versus other management programs. It doesn't mince words and it tells a very good story.

> WE BELIEVE BUSINESS CAN BE BRAVELY LED, PASSIONATELY COLLABORATIVE AND WORLD CHANGING.
>
> This is the point. It's what the Kellogg School of Management stands for. It's why we attract students who have the courage to challenge conventional thinking, who have the will to lead positive change.
>
> We educate, equip and inspire our students to build and lead strong organizations. To face outward and think forward . To become adaptive, resilient and bold in the face of unprecedented challenges and enormous opportunities.
>
> This is our attitude, the way we see the world. Our courageous and collaborative spirit has sustained our school and our graduates for more than 100 years. It inspires how

we prepare students today to manage and lead in the 21st
century. This is the point of a Kellogg MBA. (Kellogg School
of Management 2001, 3)

None of these examples go as far as you could (and perhaps should) in
telling your story in your own brand. The fact is, these brand books are not
documents shared among members of their team—they're shared with the
world at large, via the internet. As such, these documents play it a little
closer to the vest than they would if they were an internal organization
document. But remember, this is your opportunity to really tell your story,
and to put your brand in its historical, and future, context.

FINDING THE STORY

Just reviewing examples of what other brands have done to craft their
story in their brand books helps, but sometimes it's not enough. After all,
you don't get to see how these stories came to be. To that end, I think it's
also useful to show you how to take the elements we're looking at here and
apply them to a brand.

To help nail down some of these abstract concepts, I will create a brand
book for the Rubber Duckie. Yes, that very pervasive, iconic, and well-
known toy with which we're all familiar.

I've chosen the Rubber Duckie to work with because Rubber Duckie
doesn't belong to any specific company (we won't be defining someone
else's brand). It's free of copyright, and yet it's widely known and
understood. It's the perfect candidate for a brand book, and specifically this
brand book. (Besides, we have a strong fondness for all things ducky at
Paradux Media Group.)

In creating a story or brand narrative for Rubber Duckie, we first pulled
together much of the existing material that exists for Rubber Duckie. It's not
as pervasive as some of the brands you may be working with, but still, there
are enough source documents to provide context for the brand position and

to create a brand story that is, at some level, rooted in reality. Items we evaluated included:

- **Rubber Duckie origins** (Davis 2004)
- **Rubber Duckie manufacturing history** (RubaDuck.com 2013)
- *Sesame Street*'s **"Rubber Ducky" song** (Moss 1970)
- Rubber Duckie news reports:
  - Queen goes quackers at bath time (BBC 2001)
  - Pacific Toy Spill Fuels Ocean Current Pathways Research (Ebbesmeyer and Ingraham Jr. 1994)
  - Rubber Duckies Map The World (Johnston 2009)
  - The Great Rotary Duck Race (United Rotary Clubs of Eugene-Springfield, Oregon n.d.)

Rubber Duckie has a long and rich history; a story worth telling, if you will. As you read "The Rubber Duckie Story," consider the story your business could (and should) tell. Consider how to make it an engaging and interesting story. And most of all, consider how you will tell it in a way that compels your stakeholders, employees, and customers to think with fondness and interest about your brand.

THE RUBBER DUCKIE STORY: FROM TUB COMPANION TO WORLD LEADER

Rubber Duckie's exact origins are unclear, but have been traced to mid-19th century rubber manufacturers (RubaDuck.com 2013). In its earliest form, Rubber Duckie was made from hard rubber — giving it its distinctive and descriptive name. It wasn't until the mid-1970s that the Rubber Duckie brand became pervasive and iconic, popularized by *Sesame Street*, and the character Ernie's affection for baths with his little yellow friend. Ernie, in fact, was responsible for Rubber Duckie's "theme song," "Rubber Ducky," written by Jeff Moss in 1970. (Moss 1970) Later renditions of the song would be sung by great artists, including Little Richard (Richard 1993). During this period,

Rubber Duckie won the mind, hearts, and souls of America's youth, ensuring its rightful place in pop culture.

Rubber Duckie escaped the confines of the bathtub to realize its dream of becoming an oceanographer and helped to chart the ocean currents in 1991 when 29,000 Rubber Duckies and their friends went overboard in the middle of the Pacific. (Ebbesmeyer and Ingraham Jr. 1994) Some Rubber Duckies traveled to Alaska in the first year, others remained adrift for 11 years before coming in for a landing off the Eastern Seaboard of the United States (Johnston 2009).

In 2001 Rubber Duckie successful migrated across the Atlantic Ocean to win over England by wooing their Queen, with a Rubber Duckie sporting an inflatable crown (BBC 2001). This successful trans-Atlantic swim solidified Rubber Duckie's domination of the tub-companion marketplace.

Today, Rubber Duckie lends its fame to charities, voluntarily "swimming" in race after race to win prizes for its adopted "parents" (United Rotary Clubs of Eugene-Springfield, Oregon n.d.), raising considerable funds for its charities, and helping to bring communities together for good clean fun.

Rubber Duckie is proud to have provided enjoyment to countless children, helped chart the world's oceans, and to lend its fame and fortune to worthy charities. Rubber Duckie hopes to inspire fun, adventure, and kindness to all the world's inhabitants.

NOW IT'S YOUR TURN

It's time to write your brand's story. Remember to keep it interesting, engaging, and narrative in nature. Once you've got a draft written, share it with key stakeholders, and get their feedback. Continue to edit and refine the story until it's as compelling as you can make it while still representative of your actual business. Fiction doesn't really have a place here, but good storytelling does.

If you can do those things, you're well on your way to building an amazing brand. It's not rocket science—it's storytelling and packaging. Human beings are great at storytelling. So tell your story.

BRAND PERCEPTUAL MAP

I do not care what industry you are in, when you look around the landscape of those businesses that do what you do, you compare your business to the work that they do. And you have opinions about their work; either you respect it or you don't. But the thing is, you know how your business stacks up against them. You know where you are better (and why) and you know where they are better (and why). Because you are in the industry you know if they are any good or not at what they claim to do, or if they are just a beneficiary of the "old boy's network" or a random fluke.

This understanding of how your business is better than your competition will give us an important insight into your brand position. If you've got better service than your competition, then your brand might need to be positioned around the amazing service you provide for your customers. If your business is honest and your competition is not, then your brand position needs an element of "straight-talking" to it. If your business has the latest and greatest widgets and you competition uses old and outdated ones, then your brand can be about being on the cutting edge of technology. The goal is to figure out what your business is naturally doing differently and better than your competition and then to own that position.

Grant Cardone on *The Huffington Post* admonishes:

> "The concept of competition is a like a cancer in business today with companies and individuals comparing themselves to what others are doing rather than what is possible. Competition has never made a company, country, product or an individual great! Competition is not an American theme but more a communist one." (Cardone 2011)

The point is that you can't possibly be successful at the same things your competition is, because there will be little distinction between each company competing for the business. If, on the other hand, you get really good at the things your competition isn't good at, then you can create an important differentiation between yourself and your competition. At the end of the day, it's about being different from your competition — that difference is your brand.

Now, think about how you would talk to someone you respect about the differences between your company and your competition, and consider what that tells you about what your brand position is and should be. If you are not marketing your company as that, it's time to consider a shift to highlight the differences between your businesses.

Think about it: You know what your competitors really offer. You know, often better than the customers do (at the outset), what kind of service and product a new customer will receive from a business. "If we've identified our competitors wisely, we should know how our product meets their needs better than the competition." (Kloppenburg n.d.) You know whether or not the customer will be happy with the outcome, and you know whether it will be a good experience or a bad experience. This leads us to two questions:

1. How are you positioning your business and brand to take advantage of what your competitors are doing (or not doing)?
2. What do your competitors know about your business, and how could they use that to their advantage?

To start with the former, if your competitors advertise a product or service that isn't really available, your reliability in counterpoint is critical to your advertising strategy. If your competitor is great at talking a good game but fails to follow through, that also should become an integral component of your advertising strategy (assuming that your business does follow-through that is.) The point here is to **evaluate how your business can stand out from your competition, and then take steps to execute that position.**

Then there's the second question: "What do your competitors know about your business, and how could they use that to their advantage?" This is sensitive for the simple reason that it means you must first acknowledge, and then address, perceived shortcomings in your own business. Now, that doesn't mean that something they would criticize needs to be changed—it may be an integral component of your brand position and/or a conscious choice you've made about your business. If it's either of those, keep doing it! Just be aware of the criticism you may receive and take proactive steps to mitigate it. If instead, it's sloppiness, or just an unfortunate series of events, take immediate steps to remedy the situation so that it cannot happen again in the future. Be diligent about not backsliding in the future.

Let me give you an example of how to position a conscious choice you've made for your business. Say your competitors would say you are S-L-O-W. But you know that your pride yourself on thoroughness. In this case two things have to happen: In the public/advertising sphere, you can position your company as the "professional" solution or the "complete" solution, generally the business in town that will go the extra mile to make sure everything is done the way it needs to be done. Secondarily, when you start work, you need to set a realistic expectation with your customer on how long it will take. Those two tricks, used consistently, will disarm your competition's criticism and at the same time build your brand in the marketplace.

We have already seen that finding your unique niche in the market is both critical and necessary for your brand's success in the marketplace. One very good method for identifying holes needing to be filled in your marketplace is a "perceptual map." This can be particularly useful if your brand is not yet established, yet you know roughly what you do and what you want to be known for.

The way a perceptual map works is to take two concepts or brand attributes and lay them out on a graph. Then, simply place your competitors on the graph where you believe they fit based on the brand messaging to which you have been exposed. This map will highlight areas that are being underserved by your competitors and will facilitate your brand's ownership of a specific space in the marketplace. It's also useful to make several different perceptual maps to identify the one(s) that will give you the best niche, and consequently the most cost-effective advertising niche.

Creating your own category or subcategory ultimately costs you less and facilitates your long-term success. "In other words, instead of being focused on being the superior brand in an established category, such as computers or snacks, create something so innovative that it surpasses your competitors, thus creating your own category or subcategory." (Blue 2011) **By not competing head-to-head with another brand, your money can be spent building your business up—not tearing your competition down.**

While it can be a bit daunting to set out on your own course, David Aaker notes,

> "Certainly not every company is willing to take the risks of going outside the comfort zone of the existing target market, value proposition, and business model. Those who do, however, stand a chance of creating a category or subcategory in which some or all competitor brands are not visible or credible. The result can be a market in which there is no competition at all for an extended time or one in which the competition is reduced or weakened. The payoff of operating with no or little competition is, of course, huge." (D. Aaker 2011)

So if you haven't taken the time to create perceptual maps for your brand, this would be an ideal time. After all, you are getting very clear about the whole brand right now anyway. This represents a profound opportunity to capture more of your market from consumers and to better utilize your hard-earned advertising dollars. Creating your own Category or Subcategory allows your brand to get the most bang for your buck, to not have to compete head to head with the market leaders, and to identify a niche that has the potential to be valued and valuable in your marketplace.

EXAMPLES

The beauty of including a perceptual map in your brand book is that you get the opportunity to define your market, and to define what makes your brand different from any other.

The University of Sheffield (Figure 1) provides a useful perceptual map in its brand book, helping readers to understand where the University falls on the scale of "Skills" and "Ability to Improve the World." Based solely on the perceptual map, it is obvious that what the University of Sheffield is positioning itself to provide is unique in the university category.

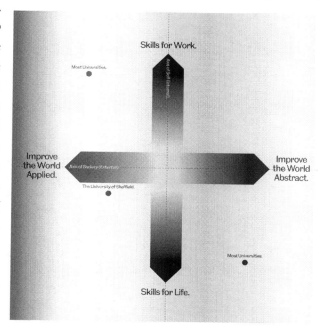

Figure 1 University of Sheffield Perceptual Map
(The University of Sheffield n.d., 5)

Ford (Figure 2) includes a different kind of a perceptual map in its brand book, demonstrating where both expectations and the Ford "Feel Good" experience lie. This perceptual map helps to define the experience as being "beyond expectation," both the emotional and the rational.

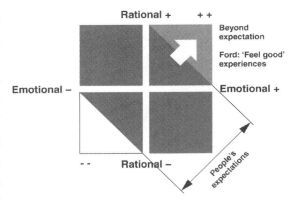

Figure 2 Ford Perceptual Map (Ford n.d., 15)

RUBBER DUCKIE PERCEPTUAL MAP

Rubber Duckie lives in a unique space in the toy landscape. Intentionally low on the technology, fashion, number of parts, number of players, and brand add-on scales, it also tips the scale on waterproof. This unique profile allows Rubber Duckie to stand out in the market and gives it a fun, uncomplicated, and unflappable presence.

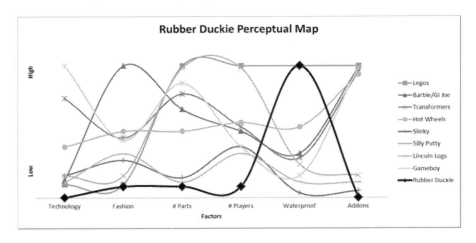

Now It's Your Turn

Make a list of your competition, and a list of the different factors you (and they) compete on. Then rank each company on a low-to-high scale for each of the factors. Notice how your company stands out from the pack. This is potentially an area that you can capitalize on to make your brand stand out in the marketplace.

Once you have the perceptual map in place, take a few minutes to summarize it in a narrative format. Don't simply rely on the reader's ability to draw the appropriate conclusions from the chart. You know it better than anyone knows, help them out. Do be sure to take the time to vet your assumptions with your key stakeholders. They can provide valuable insight that can put you on the right track for success.

Brand Keywords

Every great brand can (and should) get boiled down to just a few keywords that fundamentally describe the brand. Understanding what your brand's keywords are will help you to articulate the brand in a complete and concise manner. It can help you to hone in on the central elements of your brand.

Successfully chosen, your keywords should make up the very essence of your brand. They will be your primary descriptors for the brand position.

Examples

Early in their brand book, The New School identifies its brand keywords as Activist, Eclectic, Street-smart, Articulate, Creative, and Courageous. This delivers a very clear notion of what their brand stands for. They go on to identify what each of those keywords means, which adds depth and meaning to each of the keywords.

- Activist—The New School has a unique history of social activism, progressive thinking and internationalism. The New School has always strived for positive and meaningful change.

- Eclectic—The New School is unconventional and different, with a constant appetite for the new and experimental. Open The New School is multifaceted, diverse, and international, and it appreciates the range of ages, origins and cultures.

- Street-smart—The New School is not an insulated institution. It is part of New York City and of the larger world. The New School is urban, vibrant and dynamic.

- Articulate—The New School fosters personal expression and voice, challenging students to be in active dialogue with the world around them.

- Creative—The New School is made up of writers, thinkers and artists creating their own worlds and systems of ideas.

- Courageous—The New School, since its founding, has been a place where people aren't afraid to take a stand on what they think is right. (The New School n.d., 2)

The American Heart Association / American Stroke Association's also define keywords in their brand book although they're referred to as "brand attributes." But that doesn't change the function of the keywords for the brand. Their four brand keywords paint a very clear picture of what their brand position stands for.

> Four brand attributes are at the core of the American Heart Association brand promise:

- True.
- Positive.
- Committed.
- Heroic.

> Our behaviors and our visual expression of the brand must align with each of the our brand personality traits – bringing the brand to life in the eyes of the consumer. (American Heart Association/ American Stroke Association n.d., 7)

Slovenia (Figure 3) also does a good job of articulating their keywords in the graphic, showing the way different thought areas (sport, economy, civic, state, arts and culture, science and tourism) relate together to create one cohesive brand position that is articulated in their keywords: tenacity, activity, quality of living, organic development, niche orientation, security, everybody is an artist, Slovenian language is a value, technological advancement, selfness, and preserved nature.

Skype (Figure 4 on page 48), in a manner that is true to their brand, also includes brand keywords in their brand book. In a turn, they also include keywords that *do not* define their brand position. The combination of the two helps to create a clear definition of what the Skype brand stands for. Not only does the Skype brand use keywords that include: free, whole world, share, and calls, but their brand is also defined by what it is *not*: telephony, peer-to-peer, VoIP, and bill.

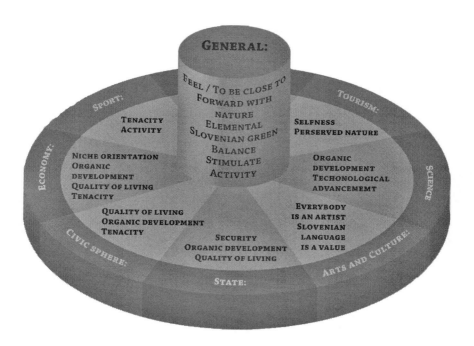

Figure 3 Slovenian Keywords (Slovenia Ministry of the Economy 2007)

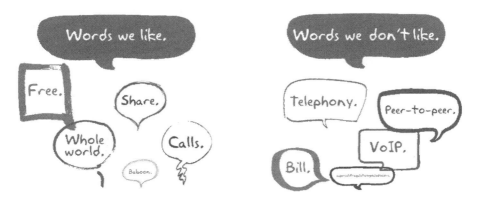

Figure 4 Skype Keywords from the Skype brand book (Skype n.d., 9)

It is clear from reading through the Skype keywords that their brand is about something different from the usual. It's fresh and interesting.

FINDING RUBBER DUCKIE KEYWORDS

One exercise I really like to employ for pulling out the keywords is to use an online word cloud generator.

> "A word cloud is a special visualization of text in which the more frequently used words are effectively highlighted by occupying more prominence in the representation. Grammatical words and non-frequent words are hidden so that the resultant representation cleanly shows the most frequently occurring words of importance." (McNaught and Lam 2010)

This is handy for rapidly distilling keywords from large bodies of text and for giving you clues to the correct set of keywords for your brand position. And the good news is, it's relatively fun, too.

To use an online word cloud generator, I like Wordle.net, copy the text you wrote for the history of your brand and paste it in, and hit "Go." What you will get is a word cloud that looks something like Figure 5 (page 49)…but for your brand.

Figure 5 Rubber Duckie History Word Cloud (Feinberg 2011)

Right away, we can see a couple of important things about the history we created in the brand book. First (and appropriately), we used the words "Rubber" and "Duckie" the most. That's good; that means we were talking about our brand, and using its name. If, for some reason, your word cloud doesn't show the name of your brand in as the most commonly used phrase, you should consider making some edits so that your brand name is the most frequently used word or words in your brand book history.

Next, you'll notice that other words from the history start to jump out at you. In this case, "charities," "rubber," "fame," "song," "win," and "race." Some of those are good descriptors for our brand position; some are not. "Fame," for instance, would not be a good keyword for the Rubber Duckie brand. Although it's famous, it's not what we want people to think of when they hear "Rubber Duckie." To get rid of it is easy, just right click on the word and remove it from the display. Continue this process until you're

Figure 6 Rubber Duckie History Word Cloud, Refined (Feinberg 2011)

happy with the words that remain as descriptive keywords for your brand. What you'll be left with is something that looks like Figure 6 (page 49).

This Word Cloud is a better representation of the brand based upon the history we've written. But it may not tell us the whole story. All brands evolve over time, and it's important to make sure that our keywords for our brand book reflect where we have been, and where we want our brand to go in the future. There are probably a number of documents that have been written about your business. Take a few of them and repeat the above steps to see what word clouds emerge.

For example, with the Rubber Duckie brand, we have the "Rubber Ducky" song (Moss 1970), with which to measure our success. When we take the lyrics to the song and put them into the online generator, and tidy it up a bit, we get a word cloud that looks like Figure 7.

Clearly, this is a very different looking word cloud than Figure 6 (page 49), derived from the history we wrote. The differences are important to note, the first being that it's a bit more of a "zoomed out" view of the brand, while the second is a very good description of the experience of playing with a Rubber Duckie.

Which is right for our brand book? Both and neither. And here's where

Figure 7 Rubber Duckie Song Word Cloud (Feinberg 2011)

we stop playing so much with online word cloud generators and put back on our strategic marketing hats. Using several word clouds you've generated, make a list of the 10 most descriptive keywords for your brand position. If you have more than a few word clouds to work from, choose the top five or 10 from each. Then begin the process of whittling it down until you get to the overall top 10. When you've identified them, they should embody your brand attributes, brand values, and brand aspirations. Try to order the words from most important to least important. For the Rubber Duckie brand book, I think we end up with a list that looks like this:

- imagination
- friend
- joy
- clean
- charity

- children
- dream
- chubby
- bathtime
- squeezable

Share this list with your key stakeholders and get their opinion. Do they agree that these are best 10 words to represent your brand? If not, what other words would they suggest instead? Collaborate with them to come to, what you all agree, are the *best* 10 keywords for your brand.

There will be many ways to display your final keywords in the brand book. One option might be to include a word cloud like the ones you've been working with to choose your keywords. Another might be to create a piece that falls clearly within your brand's personality as Skype did in Figure 4 (page 48), as the Slovenia Ministry of the Economy did in Figure 3 (page 47), or in a word cloud as we have done for Rubber Duckie. Either way, what you should end up with is a way to display the most important keywords for your brand's position in the brand book.

RUBBER DUCKIE'S FINAL KEYWORDS

BRAND ESSENCE

A brand essence, or brand promise, is the core element of the brand. It is the entire brand boiled down to a single proposition. It's the most important element, lying at the center of a brand position. It can be represented a lot of different ways. But its inclusion is critical to a brand book.

Clearly articulating the brand essence will provide context for the entire brand, and will enlist your team in successfully delivering the brand at every turn. When the brand essence is well articulated, "Managers are making changes that influence delivery of the promise, and employees are engaged and energized because they understand the positive impact they can make." (Totsi and Stotz 2001)

The brand essence also provides an important opportunity to test and to demonstrate the relationship of the brand keywords to each other. This concept is a bit abstract, but it will become clearer as we examine how other brand books have articulated the brand essence.

EXAMPLES

At Southern Illinois University, the brand essence is "Big things are within reach." (University Communications 2011, 13) Their brand book articulates not only what the brand essence is, but also engages the reader by explaining how the brand essence came to be.

> At its core, the SIU [Southern Illinois University] experience is the perfect balance of academics and access. Nationally recognized research that is making an impact. A challenging academic program for the highest-achieving honor students as well as those searching for the right academic environment in which they can thrive. A faculty as devoted to teaching and transforming lives as they are to research and discovery. A caring community within and beyond the SIU campus—one with an intellectual energy combined with a small and quintessential college campus feel. Big things are within reach. (University Communications 2011, 13)

By sharing with the reader how the brand essence came to be, Southern Illinois University enlists them in the quest to deliver on the brand essence. The university also explains how the brand fits in with the rest of the institution's ideological makeup. This is critical to providing context and a "reason for being."

Often though, the brand essence is represented graphically, by showing the way the keywords and key ideas interact together in order to create the unique brand essence. The State of Connecticut employs such a device in its brand book (Figure 8) to articulate its brand essence: "Inspiring" (Cultureandtourism.org 2013, 6).

In this case, the State of Connecticut uses the graphic to demonstrate the relationship of their keywords to their central idea, visually demonstrating how the brand essence

"Inviting... Engaging... Original..."

Figure 8 Connecticut Brand Essence (Cultureandtourism.org 2013, 6)

sits at the heart of the elements in their brand. The City of Sydney, on the other hand, chose to demonstrate how its brand essence, "Welcoming Spirit" (City of Sydney 2010, 6), literally sits at the top of their keywords and brand ideas (Figure 9) with their brand essence diagram.

Figure 9 Redfern Brand Essence
(City of Sydney 2010, 6)

How you show your brand essence isn't as important as actually having one. I think one of the easiest ways to discover the brand essence is to utilize a Venn diagram. Venn diagrams are "usually represented as overlapping circles that describe the relationship of sets." (Salton 2007) For instance it would show you, graphically, what happens in a space where A and C, but not B overlap (Figure 10).

The Venn diagram will help to force you to focus on the actual brand essence, because the brand only exists in the space where A, B, *and* C overlap. Where any two circles overlap, we're getting close to the brand essence, but we haven't fully delivered it. If you understand each of the two-circle overlaps, you'll begin to understand what makes your brand special, the brand essence, the "sweet spot", or the "secret sauce."

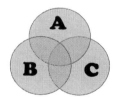

Figure 10
Venn Diagram

FINDING RUBBER DUCKIE'S BRAND ESSENCE

But arriving at a clearly articulated brand essence is a little more difficult than just putting some words on a piece of paper. To explore it more fully, we will work through a Venn diagram with our Rubber Duckie brand.

To start, we need to gather the keywords we have already identified for our brand position. If we have chosen these correctly, they will probably contain our three BIG ideas. You will recall from the previous chapter that we selected: **Imagination**, **Friend**, **Joy**, **Clean**, **Charity**, **Children**, **Dream**, **Chubby**, **Bathtime**, and **Squeezable** as our keywords. Of these keywords, let's assume the big three

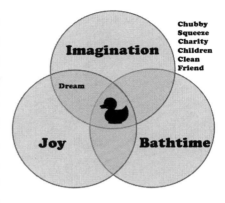

Figure 11 Venn Diagram Exercise

are: **Joy**, **Imagination**, and **Charity**. We will label each of the big circles with each of these three big ideas and then try to work the remaining keywords into their location between the big ideas. For instance, where **Joy** and **Imagination** overlap, **Dreams** exist (Figure 11).

Problems start arising, however, when we try to identify what happens when the big ideas overlap with **Charity**. Somehow, none of the keywords we identified seem to make sense for where **Imagination** and **Charity** overlap. In a world of **Imagination** and **Charity**, we do not get **Bathtime**, **Clean**, **Squeeze**, **Chubby**, **Friend**, or **Children**. We might get *Innovation* or *Fundraisers,* though—but we did not identify those as keyword brand attributes. So either **Charity** is a bad choice for the big idea...or we misidentified our keywords. A little more time and effort will tell.

Let's pick a different set of three BIG ideas from our keywords: **Joy**, **Imagination**, and **Bathtime**. A little more traditional, perhaps more reflective of the roots of the Rubber Duckie brand and not what it is evolving toward, but let's try it. We are experimenting to find the right way to describe our brand.

When we cross **Imagination** with **Bathtime**, we get **Clean** and **Children**; that seems right, although it works for **Adults**, too. When we cross **Imagination** and **Joy**, we get our previously identified **Dream**, but also **Charity** now. That fits. When we cross **Joy** with **Bathtime**, we get **Friend** and **Squeeze**. Those are both good fits, as the Rubber Duckie is a friend at bathtime, delivering joy to children and adults alike...and I dare you not to squeeze it (Figure 12).

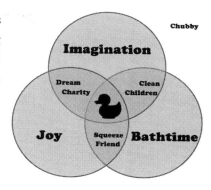

But where Does "**Chubby**" fit in this version of our Venn diagram? I know it's a key element of the brand, as all Rubber Duckies are chubby and it's a defining quality, but it doesn't really fit at the intersection of the big ideas. There are a

Figure 12
Venn Diagram Example II

few ways to deal with this problem for the brand book.

1. It might be time to reconsider our big ideas and find some that fit better.
2. We could throw "**Chubby**" out.
3. Or maybe it's *the* keyword — our brand essence.
4. We could embrace it for what it is, an important element for our brand, but not a keyword.
5. We could still incorporate it into our brand position by using a marketing technique such as an acronym. Or, it might fit later in our brand book.

For right now, we are going to acknowledge that it doesn't fit in our Venn diagram and leave it set aside in our brand book. We may discover where the word Chubby fits in with future analysis for our brand book, and perhaps we won't, in which case we will need to evaluate and edit the Keywords and Venn diagram as we pull all our pieces together for the final draft. (Remember when I told you writing a brand book could be a bit circular at the outset?)

For now, we now have a working model of our Venn diagram for the brand book. Completing this exercise has helped us to understand that while **Charity** may play an important *emerging* role in the Rubber Duckie brand, at present, it doesn't play a *significant* role, and that's okay. Rubber

Duckie got its start at **Bathtime** and it makes sense that **Bathtime** should continue to play a vital role in brand position, as it's historically accurate and future focused. It also helped us to understand we may have a problem with **Chubby**; we'll have to keep an eye on that as we continue through our brand book. The exercise helped us further identify our brand position *and* it helped to articulate our brand position for individuals who may read our brand book at a later date. All in all, an illuminating exercise.

Now it's time for you to perform the same exercise with your keywords. Remember to take it slow and to work through trial and error. Creating each of the overlaps will either work easily, or it won't. That will be telling and help to point out what are, and what are not the "big three" ideas for your brand.

Once you have your brand's Venn diagram created, do not forget to share it with your key stakeholders to get their impressions, ideas, and buy-in.

RUBBER DUCKIE'S FINAL VENN DIAGRAM

BRAND PERSONALITY

Now that we've created our list of keywords and established the relationship between them, it's time for our next step in articulating our brand by identifying our brand personality. Articulating your brand personality is an integral component of building any brand, much less a brand book.

Brand personality starts to breathe life into the brand, making it "real," as Tom Dorresteijn from Visual Branding suggests:

> "We use brand personality to bring brand strategy to life. Do not forget, consumers demand a brand of flesh and blood. The consumer will treat your brand like you treat the consumer. If your brand has no personality and no warmth, the consumer will treat it likewise: zero loyalty, high price sensitivity." (Dorresteijn 2007)

The goal of any brand book is breathe life into the brand and create tangible and meaningful ways to convey the brand personality. If the brand book is successful, it will help those who will be carrying out the brand to do so consistently and appropriately, across individuals, departments, locations, and throughout the company.

EXAMPLES

Articulating the brand personality isn't easy. When we think of individual personality types, we think of characteristics such as fun, outgoing, shy, bookish, geeky, and daring. But choosing a personality type for a brand is a little more difficult. Nonetheless, "Research has suggested that having a well-established brand personality could be a competitive advantage, particularly in sustaining brand loyalty." (Asperin 2007, 64) This is why so many well-established brands, and smart startups, have taken the time and energy to articulate their brand personality.

Adobe Systems is one of those brands. Early in its brand book, they articulate both what the benefit of having a consistent brand personality is, and what the brand personality is for Adobe.

> The brand personality describes the tone and manner of the Adobe brand that we want to communicate, in both the things we say and also in the interactions we have with customers and other key audiences.
>
> • Exceptional—We're committed to creating the best products and services: "At Adobe, good enough is not good enough."
>
> • Involved—We are inclusive and open with our customers and the communities we serve.
>
> • Genuine—We're sincere, trustworthy and reliable.
>
> • Innovative—We are highly creative and strive to accomplish things in a manner that no one has done before. (Adobe Systems Inc. 2010, 3)

The New School also articulates its brand personality in the first few pages of its brand book. It's done in a way that's entirely different from Adobe Systems, yet true to the brand position. Notice the differences between The New School's personality and that of Adobe Systems:

- Activist—The New School has a unique history of social activism, progressive thinking and internationalism. The New School has always strived for positive and meaningful change.

- Eclectic—The New School is unconventional and different, with a constant appetite for the new and experimental.

- Open—The New School is multifaceted, diverse, and international, and it appreciates the range of ages, origins and cultures.

- Street-smart—The New School is not an insulated institution. It is part of New York City and of the larger world. The New School is urban, vibrant and dynamic.

- Articulate—The New School fosters personal expression and voice, challenging students to be in active dialogue with the world around them.

- Creative—The New School is made up of writers, thinkers and artists creating their own worlds and systems of ideas.

- Courageous—The New School, since its founding, has been a place where people aren't afraid to take a stand on what they think is right. (The New School n.d., 2)

As detailed as The New School's brand personality is, the University of Alaska opts instead for brevity.

> UAF is sociable, engaging, stimulating, down-to-earth and always game. (University of Alaska Fairbanks 2012)

Ultimately, there is no right or wrong way to express a brand personality. The important thing is to express it.

FINDING RUBBER DUCKIE'S BRAND PERSONALITY

Deciding what your brand's personality is can be difficult. Happily, there is a useful body of research that we can tap into in order to help. When Jennifer Aaker published *Dimensions of a Brand Personality* (J. L. Aaker 1997), she gave us a model to be able to readily, and relatively easily, differentiate a brand's personality. Her research identified five primary dimensions for brand personality: Sincerity, Excitement, Competence, Sophistication, and Ruggedness. Aaker suggests that there are a set number of facets for each of these dimensions, and a set number of traits for each facet. The sum total of which clearly articulates a unique brand personality.

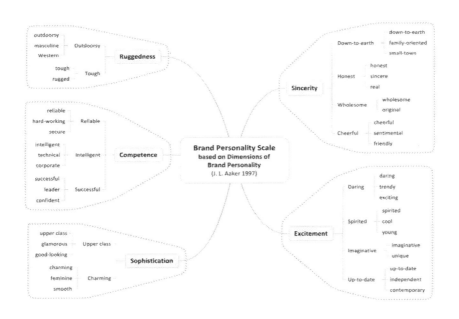

Aaker's work makes our job of identifying our brand's personality for the brand book much easier, although it should be noted that this scale is culturally specific to the United States (Anandkumar and George 2011, 34). If you're dealing with an international brand, be aware that the translations may not be straightforward. If you're dealing with a U.S. brand though, using this model, all you'll need to do is to choose which definition of a given dimension best fits your brand and you will arrive at a clearly articulated brand personality.

Working through the analysis process with the Rubber Duckie brand should help you to apply the model to your own brand. To begin, we simply start with the first dimension and choose which facet most closely applies.

Ruggedness. Our choices in the dimension of Ruggedness are limited to "Outdoorsy" or "Tough." We will need to choose the one that fits our brand the best.

Happily, this is a fairly easy set of facets to choose between. Our Rubber Duckie brand is clearly more about "Tough" than "Outdoorsy." While Rubber Duckie is an intrepid explorer, sailing the ocean blue, it's more regularly thought of navigating the interior of a bathtub, but doing in a reasonably indestructible manner.

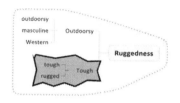

Figure 13 Rubber Duckie Personality Ruggedness Scale

Rubber Duckie, by its very construction, is also "Rugged." It withstands squeezing, smashing, and mutilation before bouncing back to its original unflappable self. "Tough" is its level of Ruggedness.

Sophistication. Our choices in the Sophistication dimension are "Upper Class" or "Charming." The inherent attribution for Rubber Duckie is simply "Charming." It's engaging, it's winning, it's immediately captivating, and it's smooth. While it's true that it has had its brushes with the "Upper Class" and even spent some quality time with the Queen,

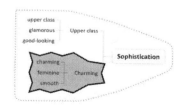

Figure 14 Rubber Duckie Personality Sophistication Scale

it has always remained true to its intrepid self. Charm is the Rubber Duckie's hallmark, and "Charming" is its level of Sophistication.

Competence. Choices on the Competence dimension are a bit more difficult to discern, including "Reliable," "Intelligent," or "Successful." Starting with the easy one, Rubber Duckie has never claimed to be a big thinker. "Intelligent" is generally not a word we would use to describe it.

Figure 15 Rubber Duckie Personality Competence Scale

"Successful" Rubber Duckie has been, no question, but more than that, you can count on Rubber Duckie. It is "Reliable." Its reliability is a key element to the brand. It's quiet, thoughtful, amiable, and always ready for bathtime. It's secure in who and what it is—a bath toy. "Reliable" is the Rubber Duckie's level of Competence.

Excitement. Aaker gives us four choices in the excitement dimension: "Daring," "Spirited," "Imaginative," or "Up-to-Date." This dimension is a little more difficult to pin down, but a couple can be eliminated pretty quickly. "Daring" the Rubber Duckie is not. Occasionally fashionable, rarely trendy—those moments of high style had more to do its position as a cultural icon than any overt effort on Rubber Duckie's part. "Spirited" is another we can eliminate easily. While not exactly on a spectrum, "Reliable" and "Spirited" tend to contradict each other.

"Up-to-Date" and "Imaginative," however, cause us more trouble. At its heart, Rubber Duckie is "Imaginative" through its inspiration of countless imaginations. It exists to help visualize

Figure 16 Rubber Duckie Personality Excitement Scale

dreams, hopes, and adventures, in the tub and out. It is unique.

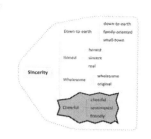

Rubber Duckie is also "Up-to-Date," although to a slightly lesser degree. Our daring Rubber Duckie is independent. It dreams bold dreams, daring dreams, and is quite courageous. Note that as the brand has been defined thus far, "Up-to-Date" takes place through the quality of "Imaginative," helping us identify the true

Figure 17 Rubber Duckie Personality Sincerity Scale

lead dimension. (One of the main ideas we chose in our Venn diagram was Imagination—a coincidence? I think not!) So that leaves "Imaginative" as Rubber Duckie's level of Excitement and "Up-to-Date" as a strong secondary position.

Sincerity. Aaker gives us another four possibilities for the Sincerity dimension: "Down to Earth," "Honest," "Wholesome," or "Cheerful." This is probably the most difficult dimension to pin down (for most brands) and specifically for the Rubber Duckie brand, because at its heart, the Rubber Duckie is about sincerity. While Rubber Duckie is undeniably "Down-to-Earth" and "Honest", those qualities pale in comparison to the next two, "Wholesome and "Cheerful."

Rubber Duckie may be the very definition of "Wholesome." There is no room in the Rubber Duckie brand position for anything but good clean fun. Let's face it; Rubber Duckie is no Barbie, either in figure or personality.

The Rubber Duckie is mostly "Cheerful," however. It's a sentimental favorite. The Rubber Duckie exists to bring a smile to faces, its squeak exists to broaden that smile, and its entire existence comes down to a simple idea: "Joy." (Yes, that is another main idea from our Venn diagram for the brand book, still not a coincidence.) In our final dimension, "Cheerful" is the clear winner, with "Wholesome" as a strong runner-up.

RUBBER DUCKIE'S FINAL BRAND PERSONALITY

The Rubber Duckie brand personality is: Cheerful, Imaginative, Reliable, Charming, and Tough. These personality dimensions help us to "put a face" on the Rubber Duckie and help to inform us about its personality. It is a personality unique to the Rubber Duckie, and with this description, we can fully understand how the Rubber Duckie should behave in the world. You can choose to display the brand personality either in Aaker's diagram, or in another manner of your choosing.

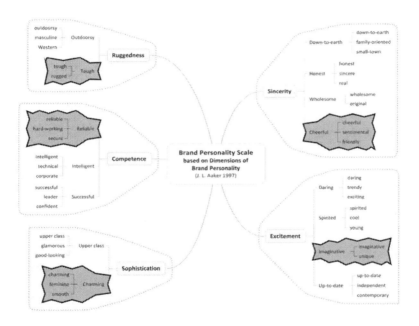

NOW IT'S YOUR TURN

Apply Aaker's model to your brand and see what it will tell you about your brand's personality. Once you've done that, take this opportunity to share the brand position with your stakeholders (investors, management, employees, key customers). Be sure to explain what it is, what it means, and why you think it's the right position. Share with them why you think it will resonate with your customers and potential customers, and most importantly, how you imagine they can help to make it successful. This is the fun part of sharing the new brand with stakeholders. If you've found the right brand, it will create energy and rally your company around the single vision.

It's critical to note that "focusing on merely establishing the personality is not enough, it must be able to give consumers something they can relate to." (Asperin 2007, 64) That means that this is also a great opportunity to tap into the collective creativity among the stakeholders in your organization and imagine all the different ways to implement your brand position and tagline into everyday business. Consider, for example, what your brand position says about:

- How you serve your customers? (fast, friendly, efficient, fun, relaxed?)
- The way your business looks? (clean, engaging, humorous, retro?)
- The way your phone is answered? (first ring, cheerfully, opening phrase, automated menu?)
- How involved you are in your community? (volunteer support, monetary support, not involved?)

If you still like the brand position, in light of what it will dictate about how you do your business, congratulations: You've found your new brand! Everything else is just implementation.

BRAND VALUES

Brand values form not only the backbone of your business but serve as a matrix for all manner of decisions throughout all levels of the organization. This can provide a powerful multiplicative effect. The effect itself "enables the brand to provide the cohesive force that guides key activities—such as product development, customer service, sales and operations—and supports the strategic management process." (Harter, et al. 2005)

You may be thinking, "But how is this different than the brand personality?" That's a very fair (and relevant) question. The reality is that, "The values a brand is associated with can also be a source of brand personality associations, and vice versa." (Franzen and Moriarty 2009, 244) They are different, subtly so. The brand values can even be different than the company's guiding values, although they cannot be disparate.

There can't be too many values in place. The reality is that the most data an average person can hold and process at any given time is "seven, plus or minus two." (Miller 1956) In other words, between five and nine separate things. That's it. That's why (until recently) phone numbers in the U.S. were seven digits long. And even with the recent arrival of 10-digit dialing, we're holding the area code usually as a discrete number, followed by seven digits.   It's simply harder for our brains to hold more than that in consciousness at any given time.

> "Powerful brands are built on a low number of values, since staff find it difficult to remember a large number of values and become unsure about how they should act in particular situations, thereby leading to brand inconsistency." (De Chernatony 2001, 36)

EXAMPLES

This will become clearer as we examine some real-life examples. To start with, let's look at the brand values for British Airways. In their brand book, they list six brand values that express the company's unique character:

> Our brand values act as a reality-check which helps us to ensure that design, photographic and written communications express the unique character of British Airways. Every piece of work needs to encapsulate and express something of each value, and should not contradict these values under any circumstances.
>
> 1. Safe and secure—Safety and security underpins everything we do Trusted by our customers and our colleagues
>
> 2. Responsible—Behave in a responsible way towards our customers, colleagues and investors.   A well led and managed British company.   A socially and environmentally responsible business.
>
> 3. British—We build on our heritage but move with the times. We represent the Best of British. We value diversity.
>
> 4. Professional—Professional approach to everything we use our expertise well. Committed to consistent high standards.
>
> 5. Warm—We are always warm and welcoming. Open and honest to all our customers, colleagues and partners.

6. Thoughtful—Understand and anticipate needs of customers and colleagues. Find insightful, innovative and appropriate solutions. (British Airways 2007, 7)

This articulation clearly helps to provide a behavior filter for staff and executives; it's *uniquely* British Airways. Of a similar nature, but also uniquely their own, Diebold Incorporated's values are concise:

Our values reflect our core ideologies and drive the decisions we make. Our values are:

1. Integrity. We are open, honest and responsible for following through on our commitments.

2. Collaboration. We seek opportunities to partner with customers, fellow associates and suppliers.

3. Innovation. We nurture creative thinking that adds value.

4. Knowledge. We encourage continuous development of our skills and expertise to better serve our customers.

These values statements reflect what we must live, breathe and reflect in all our daily activities. They are the guidelines for driving every associates' day-to-day decision making and are the tools to help bring the brand to life. (Diebold, Incorporated 2012, 7)

What I think is most interesting, just among these two businesses, is the profoundly different nature of the business the similar values describe. The same should be true for your company. The values you choose should uniquely and accurately describe the business.

FINDING RUBBER DUCKIE'S BRAND VALUES

For the Rubber Duckie brand, we're going to start by looking back at the keywords we chose (page 52). They were: Imagination, Friend, Joy, Clean, Charity, Children, Dream, Chubby, Bathtime, and Squeezable. Now obviously, not all of these are appropriate as brand values. But some are. Keywords that are in contention for brand values include: Imagination, Friendship, Joy Cleanliness, Charity, and Dream(ers).

These are pretty good brand values for Rubber Duckie. If we had guiding corporate values for Rubber Duckie, this would be the time to bring them in and evaluate them as well. But since Rubber Duckie isn't a real company, we don't have that luxury. We do have the brand essence (page 60) that may provide additional guidance. In that, we determined the big three ideas were *imagination, joy,* and *bathtime.*

Happily, two of the three are also potential brand values we identified from the keywords: imagination and joy. While we may value bathtime, it doesn't feel like it rises to the same level of brand value as imagination and joy. That means that the consideration set right now for brand values include: **imagination, friendship, joy cleanliness, charity,** and **dreamers.** That is six values, within our target range of 5-9. Those six values are congruent with the work we have already done for the Rubber Duckie brand. It is possible (as is true with all of the exercises in the pursuit of a brand book) that future exercises will provide additional brand value possibilities. But for right now, let's go with these six values.

RUBBER DUCKIE'S FINAL BRAND VALUES

Every representation of Rubber Duckie must be performed in accordance with the following brand values. They are our compass and our guide for viewing the world through Rubber Duckie's eyes:

- **Imagination.** Our goal is to foster and grow unrealized ideas, possibilities, desires, and wild hairs into fully-fledged realities.
- **Friendship.** Be a friend. Everybody in the world needs more friends.
- **Joy.** We foster fun at every opportunity and share it in every interaction.
- **Cleanliness.** Clean is good. Unclean is stinky. Don't be stinky.

- **Charity**. Help according to your means, help according to your time, but help.
- **Dreamers**. In the words of that great duck, John Lennon, "You may say I'm a dreamer / But I'm not the only one / I hope someday you'll join us / And the world will live as one." (Lennon 1971)

NOW IT'S YOUR TURN

The way to best start is simply to start. Gather your corporate values, you brand keywords, behavior principles, and whatever else describes the things that your company values. Once you have them gathered, pick the ones that are the right set for the brand.

Then it's just a matter of describing what you mean by each of those words in a way that would make sense to someone who doesn't have your depth of understanding about your brand.

Of course, this is also a great opportunity to get feedback from your stakeholders on those brand values. Be sure to ask for the feedback and invite the conversation. Doing so will make your job of getting the final version of the brand book approved that much easier.

BRAND MANIFESTO

What's your claim to fame? How is your brand memorable in your community? Are you the go-to business for sponsoring non-profits, either monetarily or with volunteers? Do you have a big annual blowout sale? Do you get wacky at Halloween or St. Patrick's Day? A crazy sports fan? Brand is all about personality, and personalities are memorable.

It doesn't really matter why your brand is memorable (well, okay, it has to be positive, or at least not offensive). But memorability counts. I used to work for a financial company that was well known for our crazy car sales in July, and I mean crazy! They would pick a theme, say, the Swiss Alps (no, I do not know where they got the themes), and everyone on staff would have to dress up in costumes like you might find in the Alps (cows, mountaineers) for two weeks straight. Naturally, there would be cowbells at every desk that had to be rung periodically, and who could forget the free Swiss chocolate that was given away to every customer? There would also be a drawing for a Swiss Alps vacation during the promotion period.

Of course, the staff hated the promotion (nobody likes dressing up like a cow for two weeks), but the customers found it charmingly goofy and were willing to play along for the chocolate, drawing, and killer loan deals. They would also seek us out at the beginning of July every year to see what the new promotion's theme would be. I'm pretty sure they also held off buying their cars for that promotion, as we did more business in those two weeks than we would over the rest of the summer.

The company became known for its wacky, all-in promotions. And it was no surprise when the local university went to the community and asked them to compete to win a spirit contest that our financial institution came out head and shoulders above the competition. The reason was simply that the culture of our organization was primed and ready to make it memorable and to go all out. Going all out was more than a summer loan promotion—it defined our approach to customer service. And the correlation was definitely not lost on our customers. When they needed a financial institution they could count on to go all out for them, guess where they came? It wasn't very long until the entire community understood what that financial institution stood for, and the business came pouring in.

Now I'm not saying that in order to be memorable you have to dress up your employees in cow costumes and give customers chocolate (well, that second part helps) to be memorable. You have to decide what you want to be memorable about your own company. What fits with your brand? What does your manifesto lend itself to? What is appropriate for your personality? If you're service minded, how can your company take a stand for community service? Are you a prankster? How can you have fun with April Fool's Day?

Your brand should be an extension of your personality. Do not be afraid to put it out there. Sure, you may turn off a couple of people—but they weren't likely to be long-term customers anyway. You'll win more customers by being yourself and being memorable.

Ready to be memorable? Good. It's time to roll up your sleeves and write your brand manifesto and tagline.

The manifesto is a central element of your brand position. Because, at the end of the day, *your brand is entirely about evoking an emotional response*—we buy from the brands we *like*. In fact, if your brand invokes anything less than passion, you are missing the mark, and that means you're missing opportunity. While I work with, and talk about, this aspect of brand every day, I'm often surprised that this critical element is completely overlooked by seasoned marketers. *The Brand Strategy Insider* nicely articulates the difference brand emotion can make:

> "Consumers care about what a brand represents to them on the highest emotional level. The physical properties and functional benefits that comprise and define a brand are of less importance–this explains the difference between Coke and Pepsi, Chevy and Toyota, Apple and the rest of its competitors." (Dawson 2012)

While functionally, there really is no difference between Coke and Pepsi, Chevy and Toyota, Apple and Dell, there are massive emotional divides. And I defy you to be ambivalent about which one you prefer.

Trying to identify the emotions that a brand evokes is big business. Millward Brown and Affectiva recently announced they can now add facial expression analysis to their copy testing solution. "Brand owners can get at the emotional response that people might not be able to articulate in surveys," said Graham Page, executive vice president of Millward Brown's neuroscience practice. "By building this technology into our surveys, we can make non-verbal emotional measurement truly scalable and cost effective for the first time." (Millward Brown and Affectiva 2012)

This means that big brands now have the ability now to real emotional response to brand messages and advertising campaigns, and this is critical, for brands that can pay the price, to be able to hit a home run on more advertisements with fewer "misses."

So what about brands that can't pay the significant study costs? They have to rely more upon the gut instinct of the marketing manager, the staff, and the community to tell them when they are on track—and when they are off track.

One thing we know for certain is that when a brand exists at the intersection of "love" and "respect," it has a significantly higher probability of inspiring "loyalty beyond reason," or becoming what is called a "lovemark." (Lovemarks n.d.) As a marketer, positioning your brand in an appropriate manner to garner your community's respect and passion is the best way to move into prosperous success. This is what the manifest seeks to create: an emotionally resonant brand that is "likeable."

The solution? A manifesto is also a tool that you use internally, to motivate, to inspire, and to provide richness and meaning to the tagline. It is your "Declaration of Passion." It is the backstory. But it is *never* going to hang in the board room. At its best, it is raw, pound-on-the-table, and raise-the-hair-on-your-arms. If you don't feel "charged" as you are reading the manifesto aloud, you have not put enough truth in it.

Think about the power that could belong to your manifesto. It is a declaration of what your business is passionate about, why your business exists, and what your business stands for. It has the power to capture the lightning bolt that is the reason your business exists, and drive all the energy and power deep into the culture and every fiber of the company. It provides the backstory for the tagline and most importantly, it provides context for the employees. It allows the reader to recruit themselves to your team and, through the employee's passion, to recruit customers to your business. As if that wasn't enough, the manifesto also immediately shifts the reader to the mindset of the brand and allows the active reader to channel the brand and to become an extension of the brand position.

The manifesto need be no more than 200 words. It needs to be clear, it needs to be concise, and when you read it aloud, it needs to hit you in the gut and create an emotional response. The reason that writing a manifesto is critical is that it will help you to synthesize your thoughts and thinking about the position. It will become the document you go back to every time you are ready to create a new piece of advertising. The manifesto doesn't mince words. It's the magic ingredient that makes your business *your* business, and no one else's. It's your secret sauce.

According to the Merriam Webster Dictionary, "manifesto" is a noun, meaning: "a written statement declaring publicly the intentions, motives, or views of its issuer." (Merriam-Webster, Inc. 2011). That is exactly what we need to include in our brand book: a statement that clearly articulates the intentions and motivations for our brand — our reason for being, if you will.

➤ *Manifesto = your flag at the top of Brand Mountain*

This section of our brand book will be our touchstone. The document we go back to before we create new brand collateral, before we post to our social media, before we begin blogging and most certainly before we talk to the press. The manifesto is the flag we place on the top of the brand mountain staking out our beliefs. It doesn't equivocate. It doesn't hedge. It says it plain and clear. It's an integral component in our brand book for clarity, invoking the appropriate emotional resonance and most of all, for inspiration.

EXAMPLES

As you can imagine, with a document so intensely personal for each company, you rarely find real-life versions of a manifesto available. Where you do find them, they tend to have emanated from design or marketing firms. These firms have more to gain and less to lose than most by clearly articulating their fundamental beliefs.

One of the best examples out there is from Frog Design (Figure 18). Their manifesto is clear, concise, and it doesn't mince words. As you read it, you know in no uncertain terms what the culture of Frog Design is like, what they stand for, and whether or not you like them.

Figure 18 Frog Design
Manifesto
(Frog Design 2009)

The manifesto from Ready2Spark (Figure 19) also clearly articulates their unique position. Upon reading it you know, without a shadow of a doubt what they are about and why they exist.

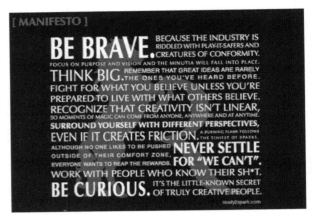

Figure 19 Ready2Spark Manifesto (McCulloch 2012)

Similarly, the manifesto from Brand Thirty-Three, while longer, is also articulate and illuminating. For example, as a prospective employee, you would know whether or not you would fit into the culture of the organization. And if you were designing a piece of marketing for Brand Thirty-Three, reading this manifesto first would put you in the right frame of mind.

We believe in the power of diversity | we believe that friends, co-workers and clients are the same thing | we believe that life is seriously fun | we believe that only wimps point fingers | we believe that words, pictures and sounds tell incredible stories | we believe age is just a made up number-if you're old, it's your fault | we believe truth is the only thing worth speaking | we believe we can | we believe that sports analogies are of biblical importance | we believe music sooths the beast | we believe in love | we believe mountains were made to be moved | we believe in each other | we believe in intentions | we believe the phoenix rising from the ashes wasn't just a fairy tale | we believe every moment is filled with opportunity | we believe in the therapy of ping pong | we believe the whole is greater than the summer of the parts | we believe negative people suck | we believe there is always a choice | we believe in the tradition of "non-traditionality" | we believe in giving back | we believe in pride without arrogance | we believe that consideration should always be given but respect is earned | we believe that nothing is "not my job" | we believe a man's word is still his bond | we believe in the teachings of lassie | we believe that healthy is as healthy does | we believe in disciplined chaos | we believe the right brain and the left actually need each other | we believe that dress codes are for the insecure | we believe character is built one action at a time. We believe in Brand Thirty-Three. (Brand Thirty Three n.d.)

RUBBER DUCKIE BRAND MANIFESTO

It's now time to create a manifesto for the Rubber Duckie Brand position.

We know that bathtime doesn't have to be boring. Bathtime should be fun! It should be a place of suspended reality, allowing dreams and imagination to take over, with invented worlds to be created and explored, futures to be imagined, and reality escaped.

We believe there should be a space where no deadlines have to be met, where no one else's needs matter, simply a place of refuge for the soul. As befits a refuge, it is restorative, inspiring, and peaceful. This is the world Rubber Duckie inhabits, and the world Rubber Duckie is honored to invoke with a touch, a squeeze, and a squeak.

Rubber Duckie is for all the world's children, no matter their age. Rubber Duckie is for explorers, at home or abroad. Rubber Duckie is for baths, and for dry momentary escapes. Rubber Duckie is, and forever inspires, playful childhood fun, and clean and pure hopes and dreams.

NOW IT'S YOUR TURN

While there doesn't have to be a format for the manifesto in the brand book, it simply needs to come from the heart. What's more important than format is that it comes from the heart, which creates an emotional response and is both inspirational and aspirational. In my opinion, the manifesto should culminate in the tagline for the brand position. Doing so both demonstrates how you got to the tagline and gives the tagline additional depth and resonance (see page 89 for more information).

Once you've done that, take the opportunity to share the manifesto with your stakeholders (investors, management, key employees, key customers). Be sure to explain what it is, what it means, and why you think it's the right position. Share with them why you think it will resonate with your customers and potential customers, and most importantly, how you imagine they can help to make it successful. If you've found the right brand, it will create energy and synthesize your company around the single vision.

This is also a great opportunity to tap into the collective creativity among the stakeholders in your organization and imagine all the different ways to implement your brand position into everyday business.

BRAND TAGLINE

The manifesto often culminates in the tagline, the short three-to-five-word synopsis of our brand position. You'll often see it paired publicly with a logo.

According to the Merriam Webster Dictionary, a Tagline is "a reiterated phrase identified with an individual, group, or product." (Merriam-Webster, Inc. 2011) This is the phrase that, after time, will trigger your entire brand position in the consumer's memory.

The tagline is what we share with our friends, bosses, enemies, and stakeholders showing off the accomplishment we made climbing to the top of our brand mountain through the manifesto. Since no one wants to be the person with a photograph of every leaf on the way up to the top, the tagline is the best, most succinct and most memorable image from the trip. It will be what we use on business cards, advertisements, and as our call to action whenever we need or want to invoke our brand position. The tagline is the public face of our brand in our brand book.

> *Tagline = a photograph of the flag at the top of Brand Mountain*

EXAMPLES

We all see tagline examples everyday:

- "Just Do It."
- "We try harder."
- "Think different."

The U.S. Fish and Wildlife Service's Brand Manual describes both the reasoning for, and the explanation of how, the tagline is to be used in one nice, concise statement.

> In the flood of communication messages that bombard the public every day, the "Stop Aquatic Hitchhikers!"™ will project an image that is clear, consistent, easily recognized and remembered, and it will be reflected by the high quality of its program components. To diverge in any way from the established specifications undermines the intent to present the campaign to the world as a unified, firstclass operation. (U.S. Fish and Wildlife Service Division of Environmental Quality Branch of Invasive Species 2002)

Getting an appropriate level of understanding for the tagline on a less than established brand often requires a bit of explanation. The Jamaica Tourist Board did a nice job of explaining its tagline concept in its brand manual.

> Our big idea was the development of a brand idea called *Once you go, you know*. The core of this idea is expressed in the insight that "there's more to Jamaica. Jamaica makes you feel more alive. Jamaica will remind you how to live every day."

> *Once you go, you know* is a powerful expression of what truly sets Jamaica apart from competing destinations in the Caribbean region. The sum of Jamaica's people and natural beauty, historic culture and unique foods, reggae sounds and rhythms, lyrical language and experiences simply cannot be

captured in one phrase or even one image. It is something that must be experienced to be understood, a promise almost too large to be believed.

Once you go, you know speaks to this experience. An almost inexpressible, somewhat spiritual journey that stays with you forever and makes you want to share with others with the same spirit...to share what you now "know" that you are "in" on the secret.

Those who come to Jamaica are permanently touched by Jamaica. And everyone who will come is sure to be touched as well. Sure to have a memorable, once-in-a-lifetime experience that will stay with them forever. (Jamaica Tourist Board n.d.)

As illuminating as the description above is, you don't have to create an additional explanation for the tagline. With the manifesto, you have already created the ultimate description. And the power you can attain by placing the tagline at the conclusion of the manifesto is significant. By doing so, you are able to drive home the point of the manifesto in a strong, powerful manner, as Travel Yukon did in Figure 20.

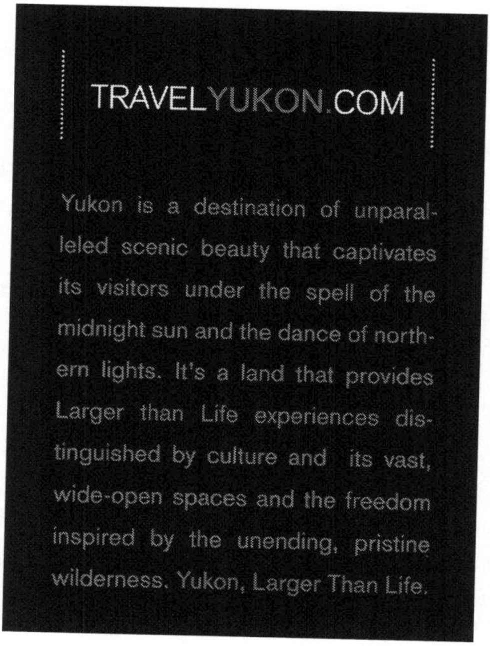

Completed taglines are a thing of beauty. But the process of finding and creating the right tagline is often, as the saying goes, like making sausage. Hang in there—the tagline is attainable,

TRAVELYUKON.COM

Yukon is a destination of unparalleled scenic beauty that captivates its visitors under the spell of the midnight sun and the dance of northern lights. It's a land that provides Larger than Life experiences distinguished by culture and its vast, wide-open spaces and the freedom inspired by the unending, pristine wilderness. Yukon, Larger Than Life.

Figure 20 Yukon Manifesto & Tagline (Kobayashi 2012)

and on the other side is a thing of beauty.

A great place to start on building our new Rubber Duckie tagline is to review all the work we've done thus far, culminating with the manifesto (page 85). Our goal is to end the manifesto with our tagline, so that what we end up with is the cherry on top of the sundae, or the exclamation point at the end of the paragraph.

Once you've reviewed all the material, it's time to start brainstorming. Block out some time, and invite co-workers to participate. Remember, in brainstorming, there are no bad ideas—so write *everything* down. You never know when a "bad idea" might be the nugget for a great idea.

The brainstorm list for Rubber Duckie that we generated has some pretty bad ideas on it, but also some pretty good ones. Judge for yourself:

- Let's bounce
- Better than plastic
- Float your troubles away
- World of pure imagination
- Childlike wonder
- Life through a child's eyes
- Float on your dreams
- Uncomplicate your world
- Escape your cares
- You're a generous one
- Float to your perfect place
- World of your dreams
- Creating your dreams
- Going with the flow
- My squishy friend

- More than bathtime fun
- Bathtime and beyond
- Cuter version of life
- Life more imaginable
- Your fairy god-duck
- Life more joyous
- Where life & dreams meet
- Where life = dreams
- Finding dreams
- Your dreams realized
- Better than self-medicating
- Escapism at its finest
- Your happy place
- Childhood rekindled
- Dreams rekindled

As you can see, there are some ideas up there that just aren't going to work. But as you can also see, some ideas spurred other ideas; that's the nature of brainstorming. There also isn't yet a clear winner up on this board, although there are some good stabs. Our experience of not finding the tagline right off is typical. A good tagline often takes some time to develop—even for a team used to working creatively and without agenda.

Our team took a break for the remainder of the day, committing to resume a second brainstorming session the following day. But everyone was asked to "stick it in the background." While no one actively worked on finding a good tagline, we were all aware that it was out there, working itself out in all of our brains. Before we resumed our second brainstorming session the following day, everyone reviewed again the material that had been gathered on the Rubber Duckie brand thus far.

The team then reviewed all the ideas generated the previous day. We began by narrowing it down to the suggestions that were close:

- Bathtime and beyond
- Finding dreams
- Life more joyful

What the team clearly wanted was a sense that holding and interacting with Rubber Duckie had a magical property that allowed one's better self to materialize—the Rubber Duckie brand is about momentarily glimpsing utopia.

The team each did a little internet research on various word combinations trying to find the right one. Ideas researched included:

- Name for someone who holds space for people to dream
- Sacred space maker
- Realized state
- In touch with inner child
- Finding fun

None of those ideas panned out. However, as is often the result of any creative process, one team member seized on the phrase that worked, perfectly. It was a direct result of the research we had been working on. As we were deciding what the next research topic would be, it appeared out of relatively thin air, a direct outcome of the creative process. And as is also often the case, the answer had been staring us right in the face:

Imagine Joy

The elements in the tagline had been identified in our keywords (page 52). It had been reinforced as part of the brand essence (page 60). It made an appearance in the brand values (page 76). And it was an underlying note in the manifesto (page 85). This tagline is the culmination of the work we have done on the Rubber Duckie brand.

Your process will be similar and dissimilar. The two things that must be remembered during the process are:

- Bad ideas lead to great ones
- Don't rush the creative process.

The final test is always pairing the tagline with the manifesto. If it works, you've found your tagline.

RUBBER DUCKIE'S FINAL TAGLINE

We know that bathtime doesn't have to be boring. Bathtime should be fun! It should be a place of suspended reality, allowing dreams and imagination to take over, with invented worlds to be created and explored, futures to be imagined, and reality escaped.

We believe there should be a space where no deadlines have to be met, where no one else's needs matter, simply a place of refuge for the soul. As befits a refuge, it is restorative, inspiring, and peaceful. This is the world Rubber Duckie inhabits, and the world Rubber Duckie is honored to invoke with a touch, a squeeze, and a squeak.

Rubber Duckie is for all the world's children, no matter their age. Rubber Duckie is for explorers, at home or abroad. Rubber Duckie is for baths, and for dry momentary escapes. Rubber Duckie is, and forever inspires, playful childhood fun, and clean and pure hopes and dreams.

Rubber Duckie – Imagine Joy

NOW IT'S YOUR TURN

Gather your own creative team and begin the process of finding your own tagline. Give your team the proper amount of time to come up with a great idea. Once you think you have it, be sure to bring your key stakeholders into the process and ask for their feedback and get their buy in. The tagline is a key element of your brand position, and you need to be sure that what you have created has the full endorsement and approval of your company.

BRAND VOICE

The brand voice is the tone, personality, and manner in which the brand "speaks." "The aim of a brand's Tone of Voice is to make sure that the values, personality, or essence of the brand is uppermost in every situation in which people come into contact with the brand's language." (Delin 2005) Think about it: When a good friend speaks, you automatically recognize their voice, and not just because the of the way it sounds—you'd recognize their "voice" in written form, too, such as the way they construct sentences, their general tone, and their favorite phrases. The same should be true for a brand. Of course, the brand voice should be an extension of the brand essence (page 55), the brand personality (page 63), and the brand manifesto (page 79).

EXAMPLES

In order to take the cross-industry element out of the following examples, I'll limit these examples to just universities. If you've ever spent any time at a university, you know that the internal voice tends to be dry, esoteric, and above all, academic. But it might surprise you to find variance in brand voices among the following three universities—and the manner in which they differ from your preconceived notion of what that voice should sound like.

North Carolina State University does an exceptional job in their brand book of articulating their brand voice. They demonstrate the brand voice in a compelling and interesting manner. At the same time, it's clear and spells out, in no uncertain terms, how the brand voice should sound.

> The tone of NC State is one of eagerness, impatience and curiosity. There's a sense of urgency in those who are connected to North Carolina State University. We know what we want to accomplish and we go after it with vigor. We're fueled by our collective talent, pride and search for excellence. We're bold, yet down to earth. We're confident, yet approachable. That feeling should come through our words — both spoken and written.
>
> Sentences should be short and efficient. No words are wasted in speeches or written materials for NC State. The structure and content of the language should mirror the brand and be just as powerful and dynamic. Passive voice is not preferred because everything about the NC State brand is active. Crisp, hard-hitting sentences drive home our points in a way that makes people stop and take notice. The words and phrases have an attitude and confidence that motivate and energize. (North Carolina State University n.d., 20)

Although less thoroughly, but equally vividly, the University of Rhode Island does a very nice job of sharing their brand voice. Upon reading their brand voice section, you can immediately relate to the intended personality for the brand. You can also tell that the University of Rhode Island values brevity. Everything about their brand voice section tells us so.

> The URI brand voice should be a voice full of confidence tempered with humility and a wry sense of self and place befitting Kingston, Providence, and Rhode Island in general. It should be the comfortable, plainspoken voice of an intelligent friend you can always rely on for common sense and surprisingly large thinking. (The University of Rhode Island 2011, 6)

In a unique manner, Ohio University also articulates their brand voice, leaving no doubt about how their brand should sound.

> The Brand Voice is not only what you say in terms of content and message, but also the tone in which you say it. The language utilized in communication materials for OHIO does not need to be forced or manufactured. OHIO has all the components necessary to tell an authentic, yet remarkable story. All of our materials should reflect this brand promise.
>
> "Ohio University enriches the world by helping students fulfill their promise."
>
> The beauty of "their promise" lies in its universal impact. It speaks as clearly to an incoming freshman as it does to a potential philanthropist.
>
> Whether we are announcing the most recent Fulbright Award winner, a gift to the University, the latest breakthrough from a research lab, or news from an individual school or college, the promise should be part of the message.
>
> To make it work on all levels, the promise has to convey energy. It's active and forward thinking. It's like the students, faculty, administrators, and alumni. It reflects the ongoing evolution of the University as a whole. There is an organic nature to the promise. It is a living, breathing concept that is part of everything we do. (Ohio University 2011, 6)

All three universities create a very different brand voice, but one that is completely appropriate to each brand.

FINDING RUBBER DUCKIE'S BRAND VOICE

The brand voice for Rubber Duckie will be grounded in the work we've already accomplished. So first thing, let's refresh our memory with Rubber Duckie's brand personality (page 70). We decided it was tough, reliable, charming, imaginative, and cheerful. That already tells us a lot about the brand voice. But we can draw additional insights from the other work we've done, including the manifesto (page 85).

Based upon the work we've already done, we know that the Rubber Duckie brand voice will be clear, common (not scholarly), upbeat, cheerful, and very approachable. It will speak with a sense of whimsy and fun. We don't have to do a lot more work here to determine the Rubber Duckie brand voice—we simply have to articulate it.

RUBBER DUCKIE'S FINAL BRAND VOICE

Rubber Duckie is the duck-next-door. It's youthful and cheerful. The voice should include the striking honesty of a small child, and remain unaffected and straightforward at all times. Whenever possible, the voice should include a sense of whimsy, playfulness, and fun. It should be reminiscent of childhood and those endless summer days where all things are possible.

BRAND RULES

While this section is easily one of the most annoying to write (and read), it's still a very necessary component. This is the section of the brand book where you articulate, in excruciating detail, the "do's" and "do nots" of portraying your brand imagery, in an attempt to keep your brand unsullied by well-meaning, if misguided, "helpers." It's primarily used by your marketing partners, but the groups that will need this section of the brand book the very most are your own employees.

Hardly anyone ever commits a brand book "sin" intentionally. And truth-be-told, if the "sinners" were interested in reading the brand book, they wouldn't be committing the "sin." However, going through the exercise of articulating how your brand *is*, and more importantly, how your brand *is not* supposed to be used will help you to protect your brand more efficiently and effectively. This section will enforce consistency in the overall brand experience.

This final step in the creation of your brand book is to begin looking at and updating your corporate identity. Corporate ID is your letterhead, fax covers, business cards, PowerPoint templates, envelopes, email signatures,

Primary typeface

Palatino Roman

abcdefghijklmnopqrstuvwxyz

ABCDEFGHIJKLMNOPQRSTUVWXYZ

1234567890,.;?!@#$%^&*( )=+

Lorem ipsum dolor sit amet, consectetur adipiscing elit. Vivamus blandit elit eu orci bibendum vehicula. Aliquam vitae nisi turpis, quis sagittis turpis. Integer interdum, lorem id dignissim tincidunt, diam dui vestibulum lorem, eget cursus elit leo malesuada augue.

Palatino Italic

abcdefghijklmnopqrstuvwxyz

ABCDEFGHIJKLMNOPQRSTUVWXYZ

1234567890,.;?!@#$%^&( )=+*

Lorem ipsum dolor sit amet, consectetur adipiscing elit. Vivamus blandit elit eu orci bibendum vehicula. Aliquam vitae nisi turpis, quis sagittis turpis. Integer interdum, lorem id dignissim tincidunt, diam dui vestibulum lorem, eget cursus elit leo malesuada augue.

Palatino Bold

abcdefghijklmnopqrstuvwxyz

ABCDEFGHIJKLMNOPQRSTUVWXYZ

1234567890,.;?!@#$%^&*( )=+

Lorem ipsum dolor sit amet, consectetur adipiscing elit. Vivamus blandit elit eu orci bibendum vehicula. Aliquam vitae nisi turpis, quis sagittis turpis. Integer interdum, lorem id dignissim tincidunt, diam dui vestibulum lorem, eget cursus elit leo malesuada augue.

Palatino Bold Italic

abcdefghijklmnopqrstuvwxyz

ABCDEFGHIJKLMNOPQRSTUVWXYZ

1234567890,.;?!@#$%^&*( )=+

Lorem ipsum dolor sit amet, consectetur adipiscing elit. Vivamus blandit elit eu orci bibendum vehicula. Aliquam vitae nisi turpis, quis sagittis turpis. Integer interdum, lorem id dignissim tincidunt, diam dui vestibulum lorem, eget cursus elit leo malesuada augue.

Secondary typeface

45 Frutiger Light

abcdefghijklmnopqrstuvwxyz

ABCDEFGHIJKLMNOPQRSTUVWXYZ

1234567890,.;?!@#$%^&*( )=+

Lorem ipsum dolor sit amet, consectetur adipiscing elit. Vivamus blandit elit eu orci bibendum vehicula. Aliquam vitae nisi turpis, quis sagittis turpis. Integer interdum, lorem id dignissim tincidunt, diam dui vestibulum lorem, eget cursus elit leo malesuada augue.

65 Frutiger Bold

abcdefghijklmnopqrstuvwxyz

ABCDEFGHIJKLMNOPQRSTUVWXYZ

1234567890,.;?!@#$%^&*( )=+

Lorem ipsum dolor sit amet, consectetur adipiscing elit. Vivamus blandit elit eu orci bibendum vehicula. Aliquam vitae nisi turpis, quis sagittis turpis. Integer interdum, lorem id dignissim tincidunt, diam dui vestibulum lorem, eget cursus elit leo malesuada augue.

55 Frutiger Roman

abcdefghijklmnopqrstuvwxyz

ABCDEFGHIJKLMNOPQRSTUVWXYZ

1234567890,.;?!@#$%^&*( )=+

Lorem ipsum dolor sit amet, consectetur adipiscing elit. Vivamus blandit elit eu orci bibendum vehicula. Aliquam vitae nisi turpis, quis sagittis turpis. Integer interdum, lorem id dignissim tincidunt, diam dui vestibulum lorem, eget cursus elit leo malesuada augue.

75 Frutiger Black

abcdefghijklmnopqrstuvwxyz

ABCDEFGHIJKLMNOPQRSTUVWXYZ

1234567890,.;?!@#$%^&*( )=+

Lorem ipsum dolor sit amet, consectetur adipiscing elit. Vivamus blandit elit eu orci bibendum vehicula. Aliquam vitae nisi turpis, quis sagittis turpis. Integer interdum, lorem id dignissim tincidunt, diam dui vestibulum lorem, eget cursus elit leo malesuada augue.

Figure 21 Cornell Brand Book Typography (Cornell University 2012)

and statements. Anything that comes from your company in an "official" capacity is part of your corporate ID. So take a quick moment and start a list of what your corporate ID includes. You'll add to this list as you work through the process, but for now, get it started.

Remember your manifesto and tagline? Good, that is the attitude you need to bring to your corporate identity. Is it Fresh? Fun? Steady? Solid? That is the feeling you want to convey with your identity. That feeling will translate to the fonts you use, the cardstock you choose, the colors you use, and the graphics you utilize.

When you are choosing fonts, remember that you don't want to use any more than three fonts in any one document. It simply is too cluttered. This would include ALL CAP treatment, *italics*, and actual font changes; three are plenty, so resist the urge to add more!

Social network branding

But do choose something distinctive that blends both the attitude in your tagline with the look of your logo. You are also going to have to choose something that is easy to read; as this is the primary way people will contact you. Too fancy a font that is too difficult to read is not going to help someone decipher that email address without their glasses on. Once you have identified your fonts, you'll need to plan to include them in your brand book. (See Figure 21 on page 104 for one version from Cornell University of how fonts get included.)

The presence of the full McMaster logo is mandatory on all social networking sites.

The McMaster University shield icon may be used as an online avatar when needed, but must be accompanied by the McMaster University logo on the main social networking site's page.

Next, is there a graphical element in your logo that you can pull out and use to create something visually interesting on your corporate ID? Say your logo has a shield in it; consider using an outline

The watermarked crest may only be used as a background and must be accompanied by the full McMaster logo.

Figure 22 Watermark
(McMaster University 2007, 27)

or block printing of that image as a graphical element in the corporate ID. Try using this element (See Figure 22 from McMaster University) in a large size, washed out, as a watermark on your corporate ID. And be sure to include usage requirements in your brand book.

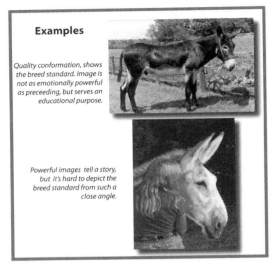

Figure 23 Photographic Requirements
(The American Livestock Breeds
Conservancy 1993)

Also try to put your tagline somewhere. This will help to reinforce the feeling you want the viewer to have about your company. Choose a distinctive font that you will use for your tagline; let it also become a graphical element.

Think about the kind of imagery or photography that will accompany your brand. What are the key elements that make up the images? Are they realistic? Line drawings? Beautiful, color saturated images that include people? Think about what makes the most sense for your brand, and then find a way to articulate it. (See Figure 23 from American Livestock Breeds Conservancy and Figure 25 from the Bonneville Power Administration, page 108.)

Once you have your fonts and your graphics, think about how you can lay out the information in a visually interesting manner. Start with letterhead—it's the easiest. Once you have the letterhead look locked down, try a fax cover sheet or statement. Be sure to include these specifications in your brand book (Figure 24 from Cooper University on page 107).

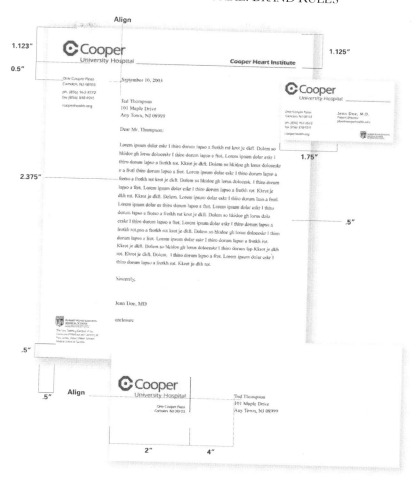

Figure 24 Letterhead Requirements
(Cooper University Hospital 2004)

Now comes the harder part: the business card. Why harder? You have to put more information into a smaller space. But if you've got a good look going for the letterhead and fax cover sheet, you'll be able to manage the business card. After that, it's just a matter of setting up a PowerPoint template (if you use it in your business). Don't forget to include these specifications in your brand book as well (Figure 26 from Smead Manufacturing Company on page 108).

BPA will leverage photography across its design mix. When used with the other design elements, photos should be vibrant and colorful, mixing technology and nature. They should be textural, and sometimes abstract and close up. BPA will build a library of available photos, using employee talent. BPA will also license stock photography as appropriate.

Figure 25 Photography Design Specifications
(Bonneville Power Administration 2011)

Figure 26 Business Card Specifications
(Smead Manufacturing Company 2008)

To round out this section, you'll need to consider your colors (Figure 27 from Diebold Incorporated), how the logo and whitespace should be displayed (Figure 28 from F-Secure), and any other consistent element that makes sense. These could include advertisements, website design, email signatures, signs, telephone answering standards, etc.

Figure 27 Color Specifications (Diebold, Incorporated 2012)

02.02 Minimum space around the logo

The logo should always be placed in a prominent position, so it appears clear and distinct. Around the logo there should always be enough space to ensure a powerful and clear visual image. The amount of clear space is in direct proportion to the size of the F-Secure logo and must not be altered.

Figure 28 Logo & White Space (F-Secure 2001)

RUBBER DUCKIE FINAL BRAND RULES

In our Rubber Duckie brand book, the Rules Section might look something like this:

The Rubber Duckie brand representation is not as rigidly defined as it is for many brands. However, the brand itself still has irrefutable hallmarks that should not be tampered with.

Our standard font is Garamond for all official communication. Letters, emails, electronic correspondence, and all other documents should be drafted using Garamond. In the unlikely event, Garamond is unavailable; Times New Roman is an acceptable substitute. Never use a sans-serif font or any other serif font in informal or formal writing.

Rubber Duckie is ALWAYS portrayed as being on the chubby side. Rubber Duckie should never be displayed as thin or "on a diet." Just as Santa is portly, so too is the Rubber Duckie. This lends to his humorous, fun, and joyful nature.

Never stretch or skew Rubber Duckie! Rubber Duckie is NOT a product of a house of mirrors. Rubber Duckie's iconic shape is a key element of the brand and should not be manipulated through haste nor intentional misshape.

Use the Rubber Duckie logo with sufficient white space around it. It requires a minimum of ¼ inch of white space around all sides of the logo at all times. Never use it behind text, over text, or through text. The logo must stand on its own and be instantly recognizable.

Rubber Duckie is best known in its brand colors: yellow and orange. While the Rubber Duckie's joviality does lend itself to dress up, the Rubber Duckie should always be represented in the traditional yellow and orange configuration—and NEVER, EVER with hair.

NOW IT'S YOUR TURN

Take some time to write down all the important rules for your brand book. Pay attention to the details. Details matter to the consistency and integrity of your brand. The more you can do in this section, the more control you will have your brand in the end. As with all the other sections, share this with your key stakeholders to make sure you're on the right track and have the complete set of rules identified.

YOU'VE GOT YOUR BRAND BOOK, NOW WHAT?

Now that you've put your brand book together, the next question is usually, "Now what?" The first thing you need to do at this point is to get your key stakeholders on board with the elements you have articulated. Share your completed brand book with them. Make sure they buy in to everything it says.

Next, put together a diagonal cross-section of your company, with many positions represented from senior management to frontline staff. Make sure they buy into the ideas behind the brand book.

Assuming you've cleared those two hurdles next comes sharing the vision with your entire staff. One of the best ways to do this is to utilize a "Brand Camp" system that allows each and every person on staff to be exposed to the brand, and the brand book, and to put their own unique spin on defining the brand.

Best practices for a brand camp put them somewhere between two and six hours in length, and can be either a partial group of employees or all the employees; however your business needs dictate. There are several components of a brand camp:

Manifesto. Share the manifesto. Go around the room and ask everyone to share what it means to them. You can do this a number of ways, either assign it in small groups beforehand for skits to be presented, ask each person to speak to it, or provide an example of the manifesto in action— whatever works in your culture.

Keep doing. This is a great opportunity to find out what you are already doing that is working well. Asking what you should keep doing will set the tone for the remainder of the session and will allow you to celebrate what should be celebrated—the places and spaces in which you're being consistent with living your brand.

Start doing. Collaborate with the employee team on what else your company could be doing to enhance your brand position. For example, ask them to go away in small groups and come back to the whole group to present their best three ideas on what more can be done to make the brand better realized. Then ask the whole group to pick the top three that could be implemented over the following 30 days.

Stop doing. Ask them what the company is doing that is not supporting the brand. Depending on the safety of your culture, you may need to ask them to write the ideas down and put them into a box, anonymously. Then, ask each employee to come up and randomly pick one of the ideas out of the box to read aloud. Be sure to reinforce that all ideas are valid and important, and DO NOT get defensive. Use all the employees in the room to find a way to fix the problem in better harmony with the brand position.

Commitment. Before you adjourn brand camp, ask your staff to each personally make a commitment to live the brand every day. (You can do this in any way that works for your company. Ideas include going around the room and asking each person to elaborate on what they will do differently because of brand camp, have everyone stand and recite the manifesto in unison, or create "brand accountability buddies" where each pair agrees to hold each other accountable for living the brand until the next brand camp.

The important thing about taking time out to hold a brand camp is to get everyone realigned to the brand position, and to give your brand the lift that comes when every employee is pulling toward the same outcome.

THE COMPLETE RUBBER DUCKIE BRAND BOOK

The Rubber Duckie
Brand Book

Welcome to Rubber Duckie's World...
Your world will never be the same.

Inside these pages, you'll find the critical elements that create the code of the Rubber Duckie. You are invited to join Rubber Duckie on its quest to spread playful childhood fun throughout the world. You'll be better for it – and so will the world. Will you join us in our quest?

The Rubber Duckie Story:
From Tub Companion to World Leader

Rubber Duckie's exact origins are unclear, but have been traced to mid-19th century rubber manufacturers (RubaDuck.com 2013). In its earliest form, Rubber Duckie was made from hard rubber — giving it its distinctive and descriptive name. It wasn't until the mid-1970s that the Rubber Duckie brand became pervasive and iconic, popularized by Sesame Street, and the character Ernie's affection for baths with his little yellow friend. Ernie, in fact, was responsible for Rubber Duckie's "theme song," "Rubber Ducky," written by Jeff Moss in 1970. (Moss 1970) Later renditions of the song would be sung by great artists, including Little Richard (Richard 1993). During this period, Rubber Duckie won the mind, hearts, and souls of America's youth, ensuring its rightful place in pop culture.

Rubber Duckie escaped the confines of the bathtub to realize its dream of becoming an oceanographer and helped to chart the ocean currents in 1991 when 29,000 Rubber Duckies and their friends went overboard in the middle of the Pacific. (Ebbesmeyer and Ingraham Jr. 1994) Some Rubber Duckies traveled to Alaska in the first year, others remained adrift for 11 years before coming in for a landing off the Eastern Seaboard of the United States (Johnston 2009).

In 2001 Rubber Duckie successful migrated across the Atlantic Ocean to win over England by wooing their Queen, with a Rubber Duckie sporting an inflatable crown (BBC 2001). This successful trans-Atlantic swim solidified Rubber Duckie's domination of the tub-companion marketplace.

Today, Rubber Duckie lends its fame to charities, voluntarily "swimming" in race after race to win prizes for its adopted "parents" (United Rotary Clubs of Eugene-Springfield, Oregon n.d.), raising considerable funds for its charities, and helping to bring communities together for good clean fun.

Rubber Duckie is proud to have provided enjoyment to countless children, helped chart the world's oceans, and to lend its fame and fortune to worthy charities. Rubber Duckie hopes to inspire fun, adventure, and kindness to all the world's inhabitants.

Ernie's Rubber Duckie Song

Rubber Duckie you're the one,
You make bathtime lots of fun,
Rubber Duckie I'm awfully fond of you
Vo-vo-dee-o!

Rubber Duckie, joy of joys,
When I squeeze you, you make noise,
Rubber Duckie you're my very best friend it's true.

Oh, every day when I, make my way to the tubby
I find a little fellow who's cute and yellow and chubby!
Rub-a-dub-dubby!

Rubber Duckie you're so fine,
And I'm lucky that you're mine,
Rubber Duckie, I'd love a whole pond of,
Rubber Duckie, I'm awfully fond of you!

Oh, every day when I, make my way to the tubby
I find a little fellow who's cute and yellow and chubby!
Rub-a-dub-dubby!

Rubber Duckie you're so fine,
And I'm lucky that you're mine,
Rubber Duckie I'm awfully fond of you!

(Moss, 1970)

Rubber Duckie Perceptual Map

Rubber Duckie lives in a unique space in the toy landscape. Intentionally low on the technology, fashion, number of parts, number of players, and brand add-on scales, it also tips the scale on waterproof. This unique profile allows Rubber Duckie to stand out in the market and gives it a fun, uncomplicated, and unflappable presence.

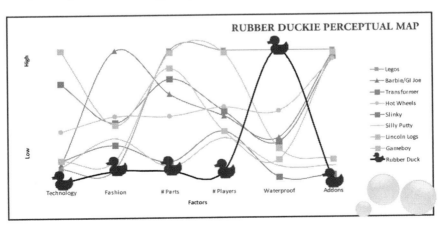

Rubber Duckie's Keywords

JOY
RUBBER
IMAGINATION
CHUBBY
CLEAN
CHARITY
BATHTIME
SQUEEZE
CHILDREN
DREAM
FRIEND
DUCKIE

Rubber Duckie's Brand Essence

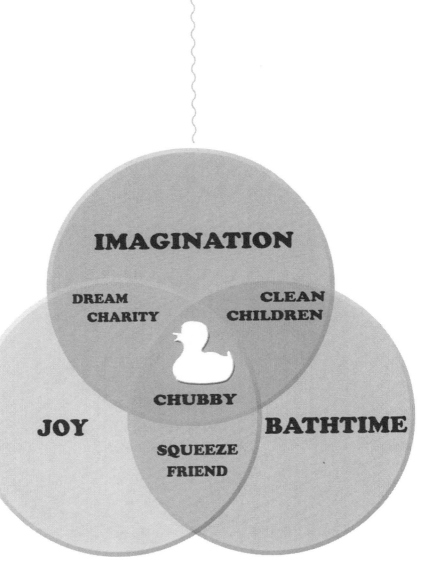

Rubber Duckie's Brand Personality

The Rubber Duckie brand personality is: *Cheerful, Imaginative, Reliable, Charming, and Tough*. These personality dimensions help us to "put a face" on the Rubber Duckie and help to inform us about its personality. It is a personality unique to the Rubber Duckie, and with this description, we can fully understand how the Rubber Duckie should behave in the world.

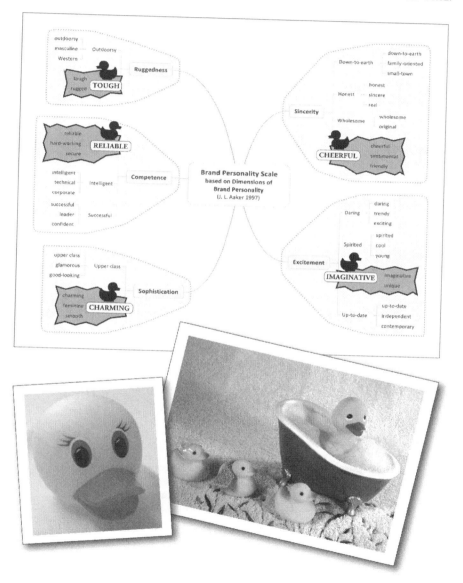

Rubber Duckie's Brand Values

Every representation of Rubber Duckie must be performed in accordance with the following brand values. They are our compass and our guide for viewing the world through Rubber Duckie's eyes:

IMAGINATION. Our goal is to foster and grow unrealized ideas, possibilities, desires, and wild hairs into fully-fledged realities.

FRIENDSHIP. Be a friend. Everybody in the world needs more friends.

JOY. We foster fun at every opportunity and share it in every interaction.

CLEANLINESS. Clean is good. Unclean is stinky. Don't be stinky.

CHARITY. Help according to your means, help according to your time, but help.

DREAMERS. In the words of that great duck, John Lennon, "You may say I'm a dreamer / But I'm not the only one / I hope someday you'll join us / And the world will live as one."
(Lennon 1971)

Rubber Duckie Brand Manifesto & Tagline

We know that bathtime doesn't have to be boring. Bathtime should be fun! It should be a place of suspended reality, allowing dreams and imagination to take over, with invented worlds to be created and explored, futures to be imagined, and reality escaped.

We believe there should be a space where no deadlines have to be met, where no one else's needs matter, simply a place of refuge for the soul. As befits a refuge, it is restorative, inspiring, and peaceful. This is the world Rubber Duckie inhabits, and the world Rubber Duckie is honored to invoke with a touch, a squeeze, and a squeak.

Rubber Duckie is for all the world's children, no matter their age. Rubber Duckie is for explorers, at home or abroad. Rubber Duckie is for baths, and for dry momentary escapes. Rubber Duckie is, and forever inspires, playful childhood fun, and clean and pure hopes and dreams.

Rubber Duckie—Imagine joy.

Rubber Duckie Brand Rules

The Rubber Duckie brand representation is not as rigidly defined as it is for many brands, however, the brand itself still has irrefutable hallmarks that should not be tampered with.

Our standard font is Garamond for all official communication. Letters, emails, electronic documents, and all other documents should be drafted using Garamond. In the unlikely event, Garamond is unavailable; Times New Roman is an acceptable substitute. Never use a sans-serif font or any other serif font in informal or formal writing.

Rubber Duckie is ALWAYS portrayed as being on the chubby side. Rubber Duckie should never be displayed as thin or "on a diet." Just as Santa is portly, so too is the Rubber Duckie. This lends to his humorous, fun, and joyful good nature.

Rubber Duckie Brand Rules

Never stretch or skew Rubber Duckie! Rubber Duckie is NOT a product of a house of mirrors. Rubber Duckie's iconic shape is a key element of the brand and should not be manipulated through haste, nor intentional misshape.

Do use the Rubber Duckie logo with sufficient white space around it. It needs a minimum of ¼ inch of white space around all sides of the logo at all times. Never use it behind text, over text, or through text. The logo must stand on its own and be instantly recognizable.

Rubber Duckie is best known in its brand colors: yellow and orange. While the Rubber Duckie's joviality does lend itself to dress up, the Rubber Duckie should always be represented in the traditional yellow and orange configuration——and NEVER, EVER with hair.

Rubber Duckie's Brand Voice

Rubber Duckie is the duck-next-door, it is youthful and cheerful. The voice should include the striking honesty of a small child, and remain un-affected and straightforward at all times. Whenever possible, the voice should include a sense of whimsy, playfulness, and fun. It should be reminiscent of childhood and those endless summer days where all things are possible.

she placed
a yellow rubber duck
in an overturned red umbrella
to float
in a captured puddle
of dreams that fell
one by one
from the sky

(Ayala 2013)

Rubber Duckie Brand Enforcers

Now that you understand the Rubber Duckie brand, you have been admitted into the elite company of Rubber Duckie brand enforcers. You are now charged with defending Rubber Duckie's brand and helping the world imagine joy. You should expect an annual invitation to the Rubber Duckie's bathtub party where all brand enforcers the world over return to share the joy they have brought to the world.

Go forth and defend the Rubber Duckie brand in joy and good cheer!

WORKS CITED

Aaker, David. *Make Your Competition Irrelevant.* April 7, 2011.

> http://blogs.hbr.org/cs/2011/04/make_your_competition_irrel

> eva.html.

Aaker, Jennifer L. "Dimensions of Brand Personality." *Journal of*

> *Marketing Research* (American Marketing Association) 34, no.

> 3 (August 1997): 347-356.

Adobe Systems Inc. "Adobe Corporate Brand Guidelines." *Adobe Brand*

> *Center.* 2010.

> http://brandcenterdl.adobe.com/Corpmktg/Brandmktg/Camp

> aign_Assets/guidelines/corporate/corporate_brand_guidelines.

> pdf (accessed September 23, 2012).

American Heart Association/ American Stroke Association. "American
Heart Association/ American Stroke Association Branding
Guidelines." *American Heart Association.* n.d.
http://www.heart.org/idc/groups/heart-
public/@wcm/@global/documents/downloadable/ucm_30506
6.pdf (accessed September 23, 2012).

American Marketing Association. *Dictionary.* n.d.
http://www.marketingpower.com/_layouts/Dictionary.aspx?dLet
ter=B (accessed February 23, 2013).

Anandkumar, Victor, and Jijo George. "From Aaker to Heere: A Review
and Comparison of Brand Personality Scales." *The International
Journal's Research Journal of Social Science & Management*
01, no. 03 (July 2011): 30-51.

Asperin, Amelia Estepa. *Exploring Brand Personality Congruence:
Measurement and Application in the Casual Dining Restaurant
Industry.* Hotel, Restaurant, Institution Management and
Dietetics, Kansas State University, Manhattan: ProQuest, 2007.

Ayala, Heidi. *Twitter @Heidi Ayala.* June 13, 2013.
https://twitter.com/Heidi_Ayala/status/345335497939382274
(accessed June 13, 2013).

BBC. *Queen goes quackers at bath time.* October 5, 2001. http://news.bbc.co.uk/cbbcnews/hi/uk/newsid_1581000/1581293.stm.

Blue, Gabrielle M. *4 Ways to Block Brand Competition.* February 28, 2011. http://www.inc.com/guides/201102/how-to-attain-successful-brand-relevance-competition.html.

Bonneville Power Administration. "Visual Guidelines for BPA's Brand." *Bonneville Power Administration.* January 2011. https://www.bpa.gov/news/AboutUs/Logos/Documents/VisualGuidelinesforBPAsBrand.pdf (accessed July 28, 2013).

Brand Thirty Three. *Manifesto.* n.d. http://brand33.com/culture/manifesto/ (accessed August 3, 2013).

British Airways. "British Airways Brand Guidelines." *British Airways.* 2007. http://www.lime-management.com/App_Themes/LimeManagementUK/Resources/brand_guidelines.pdf (accessed September 23, 2012).

Cardone, Grant. *Competition Breeds Failure and Mediocrity.* January

7, 2011. http://www.huffingtonpost.com/grant-

cardone/competition-breeds-failur_b_805573.html.

City of Sydney. "Redfern Brand Identity Guidelines." *City of Sydney.*

2010.

http://www.cityofsydney.nsw.gov.au/Business/documents/CityE

conomy/RedfernBrandStyleGuide.pdf (accessed September 23,

2012).

Cooper University Hospital. "Graphic Standards Manual." *Cooper

University Hospital.* September 2004.

http://branding.cooperhealth.org/downloads/CooperBranding

Manual.pdf (accessed July 28, 2013).

Cornell University. "The Brand Book Standards and Guidelines."

Cornell University. 2012.

https://cornellbrand.cornell.edu/downloads/cornell-brand-

book.pdf (accessed September 23, 2012).

Cultureandtourism.org. "Brand Manual." *Connecticut Department of

Economic & Community Development Offices of Culture and

Tourism.* March 2013.

http://www.cultureandtourism.org/cct/lib/cct/tourism/stillrevolut ionary/ct-brand-manual-2013.pdf (accessed July 28, 2013).

Davis, Jodie. *Rubber Duckie.* Jackson: Perseus Books Group, 2004.

Dawson, Thomson. *Brands Live in the Mind.* January 27, 2012. http://www.brandingstrategyinsider.com/2012/01/brands-live-in-the-mind.html.

De Chernatony, Leslie. "A Model for Strategically Building Brands." *Brand Management* (Henry Stewart Publications) 9, no. 1 (September 2001): 32-44.

Delin, Judy. "Brand Tone of Voice: a linguistic analysis of brand positions." *Journal of Applied Linguistics* 2.1 (2005): 1-44.

Diebold, Incorporated. "Corporate Identity and Brand Standards Manual." *Diebold.* 2012. http://www.diebold.com/brandmanual.pdf (accessed September 23, 2012).

Dorresteijn, Tom. *Outline 2: Creating a Brand Personality.* July 18, 2007. http://visual-branding.com/eight-outlines/creating-a-brand-personality/.

Ebbesmeyer, Curtis C., and W. James Ingraham Jr. "Pacific Toy Spill Fuels Ocean Current Pathways Research." *Earth in Space* (American Geophysical Union) 7, no. 2 (October 1994): 7-9, 14.

Feinberg, Jonathan. *Wordle Create.* 2011. http://wordle.net/create.

Ford. "The Brand Book." *The Brand Book.* n.d. http://www.thebrandbook.com (accessed September 23, 2012).

Franzen, Giep, and Sandra Ernst Moriarty. *The Science and Art of Branding.* Armonke: M.E. Sharpe Inc., 2009.

Frog Design. *Frog Design.* 2009. https://www.facebook.com/pages/frog-design/5612622846 (accessed July 21, 2009).

F-Secure. "Brand Identity Guidelines." *F-Secure.* 2001. http://www.f-secure.com/system/fsgalleries/pr-documents/fsec_vig_2005.pdf (accessed September 23, 2012).

Harter, Gregor, Alex Koster, Michael Peterson, and Michael Stromberg. *Managing Brands for Value Creation.* Whitepaper, Munich: Booz Allen Hamilton/Wolff Olins, 2005.

Hatch, Mary Jo, and Majken Schultz. "Bringing the corporation into
    corporate branding." *European Journal of Marketing* 37, no.
    7/8 (2003): 1041-1064.

Jamaica Tourist Board. "Jamaica Brand Manual." *Jamaica Tourist
    Board.* n.d.
    http://www.jtbonline.org/JTB/Documents/JTB%20Brand%20Gui
    delines.pdf (accessed July 28, 2013).

Johnston, Lauren. *Rubber Duckies Map The World.* February 11, 2009.
    http://www.cbsnews.com/stories/2003/07/31/eveningnews/m
    ain566138.shtml.

Kaplan, Robert S., and David P. Norton. *The Strategy-Focused
    Organization: How Balanced Scorecard Companies Thrive in
    the New Business Environment.* Boston: Harvard Business
    School Press, 2000.

Kellogg School of Management. "Kellogg MBA Brandbook." *Kellogg
    School of Management.* 2001.
    http://www.kellogg.northwestern.edu/Programs/brandbook.as
    px (accessed Septembe 23, 2012).

Kloppenburg, Pete. *Critical Branding Conversation: Audience Need.*
    n.d. http://distility.com/building-brand/critical-branding-
    conversation-audience-need/.

Knox, Simon, and David Bickerton. "The Six Conventions of Corporate
    Branding." *European Journal of Marketing* 37, no. 7-8 (2003):
    998-1016.

Kobayashi, Denny. "2012 Marketing Toolkit: How to Leverage the
    Yukon Brand." *Travel Yukon.* 2012.
    http://travelyukon.com/trade/media-kit/brand-guidelines-and-
    usage (accessed September 23, 2012).

Lennon, John. *Imagine.* Comp. John Lennon. 1971.

Lovemarks. *About Lovemarks.* n.d.
    http://www.lovemarks.com/index.php?pageID=20020.

McCulloch, Lara. *How to Build an Irresistible Brand Manifesto.*
    February 16, 2012.
    http://www.ready2spark.com/2012/02/how-to-build-a-
    manifesto.html (accessed August 3, 2013).

McMaster University. "Brand Standards Manual." *McMaster University.*
    September 2007.

http://www.mcmaster.ca/opr/html/opr/mcmaster_brand/visual
_identity/McMaster_brand_manual.pdf (accessed July 28,
2013).

McNaught, Carmel, and Paul Lam. "Using Wordle as a Supplementary
Research Tool." *The Qualitative Report* 15, no. 3 (May 2010):
630-643.

Merriam-Webster, Inc. *Manifesto.* 2011. http://www.merriam-
webster.com/dictionary/manifesto.

—. *Tagline.* 2011. http://www.merriam-
webster.com/dictionary/tagline.

Miller, George A. "The Magical Number Seven, Plus or Minus Two:
Some Limits on Our Capacity for Processing Information." *The
Psychological Review* 63 (1956): 81-97.

Millward Brown and Affectiva. *Millward Brown and Affectiva Deliver
New Way to Test Emotional Responses to Ads.* January 31,
2012.
http://www.prweb.com/releases/prwebAffectiva/MillwardBrown
/prweb9152973.htm.

Moss, Jeff. *Rubber Duckie by Ernie.* August 1970.

    http://www.top40db.net/lyrics/?SongID=70183.

Neumeier, Marty. *The Brand Gap: How to Bridge the Distance Between*

    Business Strategy and Design. New Riders, 2005.

North Carolina State University. *Brand Book Standards and*

    Guidelines. Chapel Hill: North Carolina State University, n.d.

Ohio University. "Brand Standards." *Ohio University.* Office of the

    President. 2011.

    http://www.ohio.edu/brand/loader.cfm?csModule=security/get

    file&PageID=1735272 (accessed July 28, 2013).

Sesame Street: Little Richard Sings Rubber Duckie. Directed by Sesame

    Street. Performed by Little Richard. 1993.

RubaDuck.com. *FAQ Part 1.* 2013.

    http://www.rubaduck.com/FAQ/rubber_duck_faq-part1.htm.

Salton, Gary J., Ph.D. "Guiding Corporate Culture using "I Opt"®

    Technology." *Journal of Organizational Engineering* 7, no. 1

    (May 2007): 9.

Skype. "The World According to Skype." *Skype.* n.d.

> http://download.skype.com/share/blogskin/press/skype_brand

> book.pdf (accessed September 24, 2012).

Slattery, Brian. *Simply Authentic Branding.* October 4, 2010.

> http://www.bluefocusmarketing.com/blog/2010/10/04/simply-

> authentic-branding/.

Slovenia Ministry of the Economy. "The Brand of Slovenia." *The Official*

> *Travel Guide by Slovenian Tourist Board.* 2007.

> http://www.slovenia.info/pictures/category/atachments_2/201

> 0/brand_10128.pdf (accessed September 24, 2012).

Smead Manufacturing Company. "Smead Visual Identity Manual."

> *Smead Manufacturing Company.* June 2008.

> http://www.smead.com/images/library/smead_guidelines.pdf

> (accessed July 28, 2013).

The American Livestock Breeds Conservancy. "Brand Manual." *The*

> *American Livestock Breeds Conservancy.* 1993.

> http://www.albc-usa.org/documents/brandmanual2011.pdf

> (accessed July 28, 2013).

The New School. "The New School Identity Guidelines." *The New School.* n.d. http://www.newschool.edu/pdf/VisualIDGuide.pdf (accessed September 23, 2012).

The University of Rhode Island. "URI Brand and Visual Style Guide." *The University of Rhode Island.* 12 22, 2011. http://www.advance.uri.edu/visualstandardsguide/resources/styleguide-sm.pdf (accessed July 28, 2013).

The University of Sheffield. "The University of Sheffield Brand Book, Volume One." *The University of Sheffield.* n.d. http://www.shef.ac.uk/polopoly_fs/1.166880!/file/TUOS_BRAND_BOOK.pdf (accessed September 25, 2012).

Totsi, Donald T., and Rodger D. Stotz. "Building Your Brand From The Inside Out." *American Marketing Management Journal*, 2001.

Travis, Daryl. *Emotional Branding: How Successful Brands Gain the Irrational Edge.* Crown Business, 2000.

U.S. Fish and Wildlife Service Division of Environmental Quality Branch of Invasive Species. "Stop Aquatic Hitchhikers! Brand Standards Manual." *Protect Your Waters.* March 2002.

http://www.protectyourwaters.net/resources/BrandStandardsMa

nual.pdf (accessed July 28, 2013).

United Rotary Clubs of Eugene-Springfield, Oregon. *The Great Rotary*

Duck Race. n.d. http://rotaryduckrace.com/.

University Communications. "Southern Illinois University Brand Book."

Southern Illinois University. November 2011.

http://universitycommunications.siu.edu/_common/documents/

SIU_Brandbook_032012.pdf (accessed July 28, 2013).

University of Alaska Fairbanks. "The (Official) Brand Book." *University*

of Alaska Fairbanks. 2012.

http://www.uaf.edu/files/branding/UAF_Brand_Book_9Nov201

2.pdf (accessed February 26, 2013).

Index

ADDITIONAL INFORMATION

This book is merely the beginning of a brand's journey. The journey continues at FindingBrand.com, where Tisha regularly makes blog posts about brand strategy, branding, and marketing issues.

If you're ready to continue your branding journey, be sure to join the Finding Brand Community and gain access to free marketing tools and downloads at http://community.FindingBrand.com.

Tisha Oehmen is also available for private coaching, brand strategy guidance, workshops, and seminars. Contact her at TishaOehmen.com.

ABOUT THE AUTHOR

Tisha Oehmen is a professional brand strategist and a leader in the branding field. She is also the co-founder of Oregon-based Paradux Media Group (ParaduxMedia.com).

Possessing expertise in both front- and back-office operations, Tisha conceptualizes, develops, and implements initiatives to foster brand effectiveness like no other. With over 15 years of experience in branding and marketing, Tisha has successfully led large financial institutions and health care companies down the path of renaming their business.

Where Tisha really shines is in the work that isn't done. Sometimes a name change for a business isn't in their best interest and after meeting with Tisha, they are able to find the true value and equity that has always been in their brand. Tisha has a special knack of being able to communicate the value so that the CEO/Business owner can see its luster and then with a little polishing, make it shine company wide.

Tisha is best known for developing long lasting branding campaigns that speak to the heart of the business, the brand, and the community. True brand, no matter how big or small, has longevity. Creating branding campaigns that have longevity, that have a laser-like focus, is where Tisha thrives.

Tisha received her M.B.A. from the University of Oregon, from where she also earned a B.A. in Political Science. She enjoyed a distinguished academic career punctuated by enthusiastic and successful participation in competitive speaking events, and holds numerous awards for her skill in public speaking. Tisha is widely recognized for her ability to capture an audience's attention with her straightforward and engaging speaking style.

When not working, she enjoys golfing, baking, reading, and hiking with her partner, Mike, and their two dogs, Chloe and Jackson. She's also an active member of Rotary International, the Chamber of Commerce, and is a very proud supporter of the Oregon Ducks. Tisha lives in Eagle Point, Oregon.

Learn more about and connect with Tisha at TishaOehmen.com.

ABOUT THE PUBLISHER

Advertising your brand can be tough. Without experience and the right tools, getting your business out in the open is challenging. The time for traditional advertising is over. You need to incorporate different media tools for your business to grow. Advertising alone is no longer enough. Implementing modern strategies through effective media campaigns is the key.

At Paradux Media Group, they integrate the following techniques to help boost your brand.

- Branding
- Marketing
- Advertising
- Website Design and Hosting
- and Social Media

The advertising landscape is ever changing. Survival of the fittest is the name of the game. It is more important than ever to think about who you entrust your business to. You have invested a lot on your business, so do not let it all go to waste. Choose a company that does more than just advertising campaigns. Choose Paradux Media Group.

Paradux Media Group employ a unique combination of traditional marketing strategies AND internet marketing strategies to grow your business. More importantly, the solutions they offer are fit for your business. They know that each business requirement is unique and they do their best to give you exactly what works for your industry.

Contact Paradux Media Group today so they can help you unravel the advertising paradox and get back to focusing on your business.

Paradux Media Group
PO Box 81, Eagle Point, OR 97524 USA
855-727-2389 | 541-727-0627
contact@paraduxmedia.com
www.ParaduxMedia.com

Made in the USA
San Bernardino, CA
05 December 2015